Frederick Hagen
9 December 1980.

Theatre in
the Age of
Garrick

Drama and Theatre Studies

ADVISORY EDITOR : HUGH HUNT
GENERAL EDITOR : KENNETH RICHARDS

A Short History of Scene Design in Great Britain
SYBIL ROSENFELD

The Theatre of Goethe and Schiller
JOHN PRUDHOE

Love in a Village (III . viii)

Theatre in the Age of Garrick

CECIL PRICE

Basil Blackwell . Oxford

ISBN (Hard cover) 0 631 14790 x
      (Paperback) 0 631 14800 0

Printed in Great Britain by
Alden and Mowbray Ltd
at the Alden Press, Oxford

Contents

Acknowledgements

I am grateful to the Directors of the Folger Shakespeare Library, Washington, D.C., the Henry E. Huntington Library and Art Gallery, San Marino, California, and the Newberry Library, Chicago, for opportunities of reading at their institutions and for permission to quote from their magnificent collections.

C. P.

Mrs. Yates as Calista in Rowe's *The Fair Penitent*

Introduction

The Age of Garrick in the English theatre began quietly in March 1741: a wine-merchant named David Garrick took part in a pantomime-farce at the unlicensed Goodman's Fields playhouse that lay just over a mile to the east of St. Paul's Cathedral. He then joined the company for its summer season at Ipswich, and returned with it to London in the autumn. Theatregoers of the time were fond of exercising their judgment by watching stage aspirants show their talents in the most famous parts of the repertory and, on 19 October, Garrick took the lead in *Richard III* as 'a Gentleman (*who never appeared on any Stage*).' He made an extraordinary impression, and crowded houses greeted him every night.

Four years earlier he had come to London from Lichfield, where his maternal grandfather had been a vicar-choral at the cathedral. His paternal grandfather was a French Huguenot who had been naturalised as an Englishman in 1695. David Garrick's background was not wholly provincial, for in his early teens he had spent a year at Lisbon with his father's brother, who was a wine merchant. At twenty he thought of the law, but eventually joined his older brother in a wine business. His heart was really in the theatre and as early as 15 April 1740, his farce *Lethe*, had been successful produced at a Drury Lane benefit performance. Once he had made his name at Goodman's Fields, he decided to give up his connection with the wine trade,

1

and take to the stage for a living. There were some difficulties to overcome, and he wrote to a cousin to say, 'The only thing that gives me pain upon the Occasion is that my Friends I suppose will look very cool upon me.' He knew that he would sink in their esteem because playhouses did not enjoy a high moral reputation, but he went on to ask, 'What can I do, I am wholly bent upon the Thing & can Make very near £300 p. annum of It.'[1] There was no going back, for his performances now attracted bigger crowds than were to be seen at Drury Lane and Covent Garden. So he went on to play a number of leading parts at Goodman's Fields, though, in *Hamlet*, he was the Ghost and the Manager was the Prince of Denmark.

His success was so great that Drury Lane engaged him at the highest salary ever known—two hundred pounds more than he had fervently hoped to make. He remained there for several winter seasons, but went over to the company managed by John Rich at Covent Garden, during 1746–7. In the spring of 1747 came the second most important decision of his life: he joined James Lacy as joint-proprietor and manager of the Drury Lane Theatre, a post he was to hold for the next twenty-nine seasons. He retired from the stage in June 1776, selling out to R. B. Sheridan and partners, but his long connection with that playhouse did not come to an end for another two and a half years. He left money there on mortgage, and was consulted by Sheridan from time to time about the business of the stage. When he died on 20 January 1779, his old teacher, Dr. Samuel Johnson, made a famous remark: 'I am disappointed by that stroke of death which has eclipsed the gaiety of nations and impoverished the public stock of harmless pleasure.'

It is unlikely that the last phrase could have been used to describe any theatre manager who had died in 1741, but in the course of his career, Garrick had raised the stage greatly in public estimation. Restoration comedies were gradually transformed or dropped from the repertoire, and a concern for

---

1 *The Letters of David Garrick* (ed. D. M. Little and G. M. Kahrl, Cambridge, Mass., 1963), p. 29.

morality was evident in the number of tragedies and sentimental comedies that were produced. The company was carefully disciplined, and Garrick himself was on intimate terms with some of the leading noblemen of the day. For all these reasons his playhouse became one of the most respected institutions in London.

English acting had been keenly admired by foreigners before Garrick's day. The famous Italian player, Luigi Riccoboni, declared in his *Historical and Critical Account of the Theatre in Europe* (1741), 'If after forty-five years' experience I may be entitled to give my Opinion, I dare advance that the best actors in *Italy* and *France* come far short of those in England.'[2] Betterton and Booth, Wilks and Colley Cibber, had all brought glory, in their own way, to the English stage, but Garrick revolutionised the old style of playing by his 'natural' acting. He concentrated on 'turns', psychological revelation in the moments of transition from one aspect of character to another, and these triumphs of insight and technique were best seen in his performances of Shakespeare's greatest tragedies. A later foreign visitor remarked that 'the English theatre is said to have attained its greatest degree of perfection during the last years of Garrick's life; and, without doubt, this is its most brilliant period. The principal works of the immortal Shakespeare, and other celebrated dramatic poets, were then represented with a justice, a dignity, and a magnificence before unknown.'[3]

Garrick also made some effort to restore Shakespeare's lines to texts that had been partly stripped of them, though where he thought a scene needed improvement, he supplied new lines himself. He collected early and very rare editions, lent them to scholars at work on the texts, and finally left them to the British Museum. He was called 'Shakespeare's priest', and remarked that 'the next best thing to saying your prayers was certainly reading *Macbeth*.'[4] His interest was undoubtedly genuine, but

2 P. 176.
3 M. D'Archenholz, *A Picture of England* (Dublin, 1791), p. 235.
4 *The Sun*, 13 March 1808.

his work in 'promoting' Shakespeare was also good for business and for the reputation for respectability which his theatre enjoyed.

Drury Lane Theatre, like Covent Garden, had a royal patent for performances. This placed both playhouses in an extraordinarily strong position, for the Licensing Act of 1737 confined play-acting to their stages. The population of London went on growing and in spite of religious opposition to the theatre, the two patent houses were often crammed full.

They had little opposition to face from the unlicensed theatres that had to find some way of evading the law if they were to keep open. The Licensing Act did not refer to musical performances, so at Goodman's Fields the audience was charged for a concert but was also entertained with the 'rehearsal' of a play. The legal position of Goodman's Fields was very insecure and at the end of Garrick's performances there, the theatre closed down. Sadler's Wells, as a 'Musick House', had a luckier history,[5] but in general unlicensed theatres had short lives.

The smaller the opposition, the better the patent theatres were pleased, and they drew into their ranks the greatest players of the age: Garrick, Barry, Powell, Woodward, Shuter, King, Macklin, Smith, Moody, Yates and Thomas Sheridan, as well as Susanna Cibber, Hannah Pritchard, Catherine Clive, Peg Woffington, George Anne Bellamy, Frances Abington, and Mary Ann Yates.

The theatres were open on every night of the week from the middle of September to the end of May, and different programmes were given at every performance. A comedy or tragedy would be followed by a farce, pantomime, or burlesque and in the interval songs and dances were presented. The choice of items was largely dictated by the managers from what they knew of the abilities of the company. It was taken for granted that actors had possession of certain parts and, while others might occasionally take these roles as a novelty or at a

---

5 I have omitted the summer seasons at the Haymarket from this survey, since they have little that is unusual to offer.

benefit, they were otherwise the property of the people who had been engaged to play them. As long as Quin was at Covent Garden, *Henry IV, Part I* was sure to be among the pieces regularly performed and he was certain to play Falstaff.

Few new plays were acted, and the audience's pleasure was derived from the repetition of plays they knew well. Many people attended on several nights in the week and prided themselves on being connoisseurs of acting, ready to note the slight change of 'business' or inflection of tone. Garrick's 'eye' was often mentioned, for the theatres were still intimate enough in size to allow spectators to note the way his very dark eyes caught the light and suggested his emotions. Not a whisper of his was missed at Drury Lane for the acoustics were excellent and the actor knew well how to convey his meaning: 'There the dialogue of comedy required no higher tone than the conversation of the drawing room.'[6] Mrs. Pritchard, too, was a mistress of aural effect: 'not a word, or scarce a loud breathing of hers escaped you, whether she played Lady Macbeth or Beatrice.'[7]

Early in the century a character in *The Lawyer's Fortune* remarked, 'Plays are endeavour'd to humour the times, and the Company that attend 'em; and therein they have an Eye to comply with the greater Number of People who for the most part, are ill-bred Citizens, Jews, and Merchants' Prentices.' The first part of the statement was still true in the Age of Garrick, but the playhouse now entertained a much wider section of society and might well be termed a popular centre for the arts.

6 *The Pic Nic* (1803), i. 20. 7 *Idem.*

CHAPTER TWO

Acting

Thomas Gainsborough, that most observant of painters and least flattering of men, was proud to tell Garrick that he was 'the humblest of your million of admirers.' Edmund Burke, lover of tradition, was ready to argue that parliamentary precedent should be ignored to accommodate Garrick, a man who had taught the Commons eloquence. Charles Churchill, the scourge of players, almost attained eulogy in his verse portrait[1] of the great actor:

> If manly Sense, if Nature link'd with Art;
> If thorough knowledge of the Human Heart;
> If Powers of acting vast and unconfin'd;
> If fewest Faults, with greatest Beauties join'd;
> If strong Expression, and strange Powers which lie
> Within the magic circle of the Eye,
> If feelings which few hearts, like his, can know,
> And which no face so well as His can show,
> Deserve the Preference, GARRICK! take the chair,
> Nor quit it—Till thou place an Equal there.

To the eighteenth century, Garrick was the outstanding actor of modern times, and to call him 'Roscius' as was so often done, was merely to indicate that in one respect at least England could rival ancient Rome.

The hypnotic effect of his acting is well described in

6   1 *The Rosciad* (8th ed., 1763), lines 1081–90.

November 1761, on the occasion of a command performance: 'He has a most absolute power over the Queen's Person, and in some Charack[ters] makes her laugh so violently, that one would pity her royal Sides. For my own part, I can compare myself to nothing but a mere Machine Set to motion just as Garrick's Magic wills. Pity, Anger, Grief, Joy, and all the soft tumults of love have in their turn so fired my Soul, that I could safely Swear the peace against Garrick's acting . . . '[2]

At the very outset of his career, his performance as Richard Crookback had caused the celebrated actress, Mrs. Pritchard, to say, 'You did more at your first appearing than ever anybody did with twenty years' practice.' Alexander Pope declared, 'that young man never had his equal, and he never will have a rival.' Garrick went on drawing expressions of rapture and amazement throughout his long connection with Drury Lane, and we are bound to wonder what was so outstanding about him. The answer is difficult to find because in any performance the sum of the qualities that make it great is often mentioned, but the breakdown of them is more frequently evaded. Fortunately some of his contemporaries were sufficiently thorough and detached to recall their impressions fairly carefully.

What we should like to discover is a description of a performance in one of his great Shakespearean roles that goes into close detail throughout. In default of that we must accept what we can find—an account of Garrick's portrayal of Hastings in Rowe's *Jane Shore*. It appeared in a newspaper after Garrick's death and was obviously drawn from notes made at the time of performance.[3] They are only one man's impressions, but they give us a clear guide to the way in which the great actor interpreted the part.

Jane Shore held the stage throughout the eighteenth century, in spite of its conventional language and monotonous blank

2 C. Price, 'David Garrick and Evan Lloyd,' *Review of English Studies*, N.S., ii (1952), 28.
3 The cutting is in a volume of material collected by George Daniel and entitled, 'Garrick and his Contemporaries' (pp. 73–9), in the Folger Shakespeare Library.

verse. There were good reasons for its success: it was carefully constructed, one scene led neatly on to the next. The characterisation was competent and its main interest lay not in the tyrant Gloster, who lacked the demonic humour of Richard III, but in the extreme penitence of Jane Shore and the varying moods of Hastings.

Even before he made his appearance, Hastings's stubborn fidelity to the little princes as well as his breach of faith with Alicia and subsequent interest in Jane Shore, had been made plain. The contrast between one kind of loyalty and another aroused a natural curiosity. Garrick entered 'in a very gay, court-like manner', which changed abruptly when he described to Gloster Jane's 'pining in despair'. Gloster remarked that Hastings frequently visited her, and Garrick replied 'with nice hesitation and much fine feeling',

> No farther, my good Lord, than friendly Pity
> And tender-hearted Charity allow.

Gloster agreed to hear her grievances.

Hastings went to give her this news and met Alicia. Once again, Garrick made an extremely gay entrance but 'stared at seeing Alicia, and his whole demeanour seemed to change. The next three speeches were given with great cunning and coldness.' Alicia had doated on him, and in his formal reply to her,

> None has a Right more ample
> To task my Pow'r than you,

his inflections were emphatic 'but not gallant'. When she attacked him vehemently for his falseness, 'he walked up to her, met her eye fully', and cried 'with a degree of sharpness that bordered on severity,

> Are you wise?
> Have you the use of Reason? Do you wake?
> What means this raving! this transporting Passion?'

In his next speech, reproving her for her insulting words, 'he softened a little, but still kept up the tyrant.' When she persisted, 'he lost his temper in some degree, made the speech ("Why am I thus pursued?") a fine climax, and crossed in front of her at its end.' At her mention of his arts and midnight visits, 'he softened, took her left hand in his, and with the fore-finger of his right hand deliberately seemed to enforce the emphatic advice, "Believe me true, nor listen to your jealousy." ' As he came to the end of the ten-line speech with its suggestion that if she did not listen to him her heart would be pinched with pain, he 'gently threw away her hand and turned up the stage.' Alicia disdained his advice, overcome completely by his treachery:

> Ev'n now thy Eyes avow it, now they speak
> And insolently own the Glorious Villainy.

The eighteenth-century spectator added that, at this point, Garrick personified her description; and had undoubtedly spoken his lines 'with great insolence; but it was elegant insolence—not the unpolished rudeness of the present age.' To her threat of revenge he replied with 'dry, gentlemanly humour':

> Whate'er my Fate decrees for me hereafter,
> Be present to me now, my better Angel!
> Preserve me from the Storm which threatens now,
> And if I have beyond Attonement sinn'd,
> Let any other kind of Plague o'ertake me,
> So I escape the Fury of that Tongue.

The spectator noted that the manner of delivery was like that employed by Garrick in the light-heartedly promiscuous Ranger, and observed that it 'produced a roar of applause that did not seem to belong to a tragedy'.

Alicia quitted the stage and Garrick gave an eighteen-line soliloquy on the theme, 'How fierce a Fiend is passion.' He uttered the opening line 'with great sympathy and firmness', but an entire change of manner and facial expression followed, and when he described Jane Shore's entrance, the critic thought he became the 'most insinuating, accomplished lover, I ever listened to.'

Jane Shore's kneeling to him brought the response, 'Rise,

9

B

gentle dame', in the 'true style of the courtier, to make the light and shade complete'. The effect was amplified in his next speech:

> If there be ought of Merit in my Service,
> Impute it there, when most is due, to Love.
> Be kind, my gentle Mistress, to my Wishes,
> And satisfie my panting Heart with Beauty.

The spectator described Garrick as advancing 'with seeming timidity, very tenderly took her hand, kept sinking by degrees as he spoke, and just touched the ground with his knee as he said "to love". He paused a little before that line, but at the close "to love", no language could describe his manner, or the effect produced.' His next two speeches were also given 'in the most tender agitated tones imaginable', but when Jane Shore suggested he look for someone other than herself as a 'worthy Partner', a change came over him, and he seemed 'as if his pride was piqued', when he exclaimed, 'What means this peevish, this fantastic Change?' His tenderness then 'dwindled to perfect rudeness', and shortly afterwards reached 'a rapid climax of determined brutality.' As he dragged her towards the bedchamber, Dumont heard her cries and reproached Hastings with his dishonourable conduct. Garrick 'quitted her, and took the stage once or twice in great disorder before he spoke, till he came to the passage:

> 'Tis wondrous well! I see, my Saint-like Dame
> You stand provided of your Braves and Ruffians,
> To man your Cause, and bluster in your Brothel.'

He crossed the stage in front of Dumont, and spoke down the wing as Jane Shore left him. When Dumont insisted that he take back his insulting words, he received the reply:

> Insolent Villain! Henceforth let this teach thee
> The distance betwixt a Peasant and a Prince

Garrick drew his sword, and struck Dumont gently across the arm. When he was disarmed in the sword-play, Garrick left the scene 'not with loud but stifled rage, and keen resentment.'

He entered in the third act just as Gloster said to Catesby that he means

> To prove him [Hastings] to the Quick; then if he flinch
> No more but this, away with him at once.
> He must be mine or nothing.

Hastings did not notice them but spoke some words to himself:

> This foolish Woman hangs about my Heart,
> Lingers, and wanders in my Fancy still.
> This Coyness is put on; 'tis Art and Cunning,
> And worn to urge Desire,—I must possess her;
> The Groom, who lift his sawcy Hand against me,
> E'er this, is humbled, and repents his daring,
> Perhaps, ev'n she may profit by th' Example,
> And teach her Beauty not to scorn my Pow'r.

Garrick gave these lines 'unbridled expression.' The spectator noted that it was possible before this to believe that Hastings loved Jane because his advances were so tender and so earnest, and that even his use of force might seem sanctioned by disappointment; 'but here the open, gay and bold-faced villain, clearly stands confessed.'

When Gloster said that England's discontents were caused by the fact that 'the Crown sits on a baby brow', Hastings answered him with a brief speech in which 'a little of the Court sycophant was displayed in a masterly style.' But finding that Gloster was not tickled by it . . . he [Hastings] assumed his dignity and was himself, 'vehemently rejecting Gloster's suggestion that some patriot "should . . . new mold the State" '. He called a curse on anyone who plunged the country into civil war, and over the twenty-four lines his voice rose to a fine climax: 'the applause was beyond any thing of that kind now given.'

Yet he also said to Gloster:

> No, Heaven forfend that e'er your Princely Person
> Should come within the Scope of my Resentment.

The lines were uttered by Garrick 'in a faint agitated undertone, and the Courtier finely portrayed.' Gloster seemed to accept him as 'a right honest man', and left Hastings to soliloquize:

> I am not read
> Nor skill'd and practis'd in the Arts of Greatness.

The spectator remarked that the subsequent lines proved that even when mean or vicious principles were dominant, men would always strive to convince themselves they were free from them: 'Hastings has just before given the lie to the first three lines of this soliloquy. His loyalty was the only virtue he possessed.'

In the fourth act, at the meeting of the Council, Hastings appeared oppressed: 'there was a gloom about Mr. Garrick in this scene as if something was to happen dreadful; but his wonderful expression of countenance, his deep heart-felt tones on being arrested for high-treason, cannot be described.' His daring to question Gloster had prompted the decision, 'He sha' not live an Hour.' Hastings then spoke six lines that brought out all the subtleties of Garrick's art; 'this one little speech he was two minutes in speaking':

> What! and no more but this—how, to the Scaffold:
> Oh, gentle Ratcliffe! tell me, do I hold thee?
> Or if I dream, what shall I do to wake,
> To break, to struggle thro' this dread Confusion?
> For surely Death itself is not so painful
> As is this sudden Horror and Surprise.

He wept a little, 'and then a flood of tears gave him ease and power for his succeeding speeches.'

These occurred after Alicia entered and revealed to him that she was partly responsible for his sentence. Garrick omitted Hastings's speech beginning 'O! thou inhuman', and gave all his powers to 'speak and give ease to thy conflicting passions!' and to the one commencing with 'Thy reason is grown wild'. Both were 'pronounced with the wild, distracted manner of a man not satisfied with himself, and hurrying to death.' With the line 'Now mark! and tremble at Heaven's Just Award', he got perfectly calm and composed, and these lines were uttered in a deep affecting tone that was truly heart-rending; and in 'Here, then, exchange we mutually forgiveness', he contrived by a little pause, and then kneeling with her, to get rid of grief and every distracting thought; he held one of her hands, in his, while he made the address to heaven, and did it with great energy and firmness; and in the passage, 'Farewell! good angels visit thy afflictions', he left her again in tears, got close to the wing, spoke the last two sentences with uncommon feeling, and made a great *exit*. The applause lasted long, for half the house did not expect to see him any more. But he returned with his guard, went over to Alicia, tenderly took her hand, then turned and waved the guard to retire a little, which they did. He then led her farther off again as if to speak in private, and delivered the petition for Jane Shore comparatively in a whisper, 'till he came to the line of 'O! shouldst thou wrong her',[4] where he swelled his cadence; but immediately subsiding once more, into a whisper, he left her and got again to the wing. They looked at each other for some time with heart-rending grief, and he, after a pause, gave the passage, 'Remember this', in the tone of a man expiring; but I cannot recollect that he said 'Farewell for ever'. The 'last warning of a dying man' had taken such hold of Miss Young[e] and the audience that nothing more could be said or done with effect.

There was one more act to come but Hastings's part was ended, and for Garrick's admirers the supreme moments of the play were over, too. They had seen him in full maturity: the reference to Miss Younge proves that the performance described must have been one of the five in which she played Alicia to Garrick's Hastings in November and December 1773.

The recollections of the unknown commentator are clear enough for us to gain some impression of the power of Garrick's

---

4 The warning to Alicia reads:
    Let not the Rancour of thy hate Pursue
    The Innocence of thy unhappy Friend.
    Thou know'st who 'tis I mean; Oh! shouldst thou wrong her
    Just Heav'n shall double all thy Woes upon thee,
    And make 'em know no End. Remember this
    As the last Warning of a dying Man.
    Farewell forever. (*The Guards carry Hastings off.*)

acting. Rowe's conception of Hastings allowed the player to make the most of sudden shifts of mood from gaiety to brutality, plausibility to earnestness, mocking scepticism to sentimental loyalty. Balancing one extreme against another and searching for some unifying factor, the audience was held by this gradual revelation of a complex human being. Perception was aided by the way in which the lines were articulated, sometimes excitedly, sometimes with a deliberation that took two minutes over a short passage. A great variety of movements reinforced the effect of gesture and facial expression.

This seems to us so normal a method of acting, that it is important to contrast it with the style employed by some of the leading French actors of the day and of their English adherents. The technique of 'the principal comedian' of France is described in John Hill's *The Actor*, which is itself based on Ste. Albine's *Le Comédien*: 'he has less action than any of the English players: He will stand in his place on the stage, with his arms genteelly disposed, and without once stirring hand or foot, go thro' a scene of the greatest variety. He will in this single posture express to his audience all the changes of passion that can affect an human heart; and he will express them strongly: So that tossing about of the arms and strutting from side to side of the stage, is not the business.'[5] Something was achieved by expression of face but much more by modulation of voice.

In England a certain modulation of tone had been practised in tragedy by earlier actors. The preface to *The Fairy Queen* (1692) makes a comparison between opera and tragedy that is worth considering: 'the one is a Story, sung with proper Action, the other spoken . . . And he must be a very ignorant Player who knows not there is a Musical Cadence in speaking; and that a Man may as well speak out of Tune, as sing out of Tune.' Just what is meant by a 'Musical Cadence' is not specified. John Hill declared that 'of old the delivery of speeches in tragedy was regulated by certain musical notes; but what that practice

5 (1755), 73. He describes Le Kain.

was we do not perfectly understand.' He added, 'the recitation was a kind of singing.'[6] The sounds were remembered in the seventeen-sixties when Benjamin Victor mentioned 'the good old Manner of singing and quavering out their tragic notes.'[7] It went with buskins and the tragic plume, and was a way of imposing dignity on phrasing by giving it a markedly different cadence from ordinary speech.

Stage speech normally differs from the ordinary in its heightening, and the degree of heightening varies from age to age. Garrick found the French and earlier English styles too slow and heavy for his purpose, and pointed his lines in a way that broke completely with the old sonorities and was perfectly suited to his more restless style of acting. Even in the comic vein, he laid himself open to the Abbé Le Blanc's charge that the English actor expressed the humour of his part 'more by the grimaces of his face, than the proper modulation of his voice.'[8]

Hostile critics thought his contempt for the stiff French style led him into absurdities. Theophilus Cibber put the point very strongly: 'his over-fondness for extravagant Attitudes, frequently affected Starts, convulsive Twitchings, Jerkings of the Body, sprawling of the Fingers, flapping the Breast and Pockets: —A Set of mechanical Motions in constant Use—the Caricatures of Gesture, suggested by pert Vivacity,—his pantomimical Manner of acting, every Word in a Sentence, his Unnatural Pauses in the middle of a Sentence; his forc'd Conceits;—his wilful Neglect of Harmony, even where the round Period of a well express'd Noble Sentiment demands a graceful Cadence in the delivery.'[9] David Williams was less offensive: 'Your perfection consists *in the extreme*; in exaggerated gesture, and sudden bursts of passion, given in a suppressed and under manner, where the extensive powers of voice are not required; you are inimitable. In the struggles and conflicts of contra-

[6] *Op. cit.*, pp. 241, 239.
[7] *The History of the Theatres of London and Dublin* (1761), ii. 164. Cf. A. C. Sprague, 'Did Betterton Chant,' *Theatre Notebook*, i (1946), 54–5.
[8] *Letters on the English and French Nations* (1747), ii. 42.
[9] *Two Dissertations on the Theatres* (1756), p.56.

15

dictory passions; or in their mixture and combination; and when their effects are drawn by the author to a point of instant and momentary expression;—there you are often excellent. But where the situation of the mind implies a continued agitation, you become defective. And in all simple, unmixed passions, in all the simpler degrees of expression; and in conveying the *various* proportion of pathos which various cases require; in these cases you are no longer *yourself*, the expression must be *in extreme*, or you are not *Garrick* ... In all degrees below the extreme, your gesture, and every species of expression, is what the French call *trop chargé*. . . .'[10]

The strictures were too laboured, but they revealed the strength of Garrick's reaction against the French style. Instead of standing still so that his voice could entirely hold the audience's attention, he set off his words with appropriate action, gesture, and miming that approximated as far as possible to an everyday disclosure of the feelings. Elevation was achieved not through relentless grandeur of sound but by revealing that certain actions and gestures were true to human nature in a particular set of circumstances. As one writer put it, 'Garrick, indeed, corrected the audience's taste: he taught them, by the greatness of his acting, to know those nice touches of nature, which they were till then strangers to. When he acted, the audience saw what was right.'[11]

What then is 'nature' and how can it be revealed? The problem is discussed in some verse of the time:

> Our guide is Nature;—that is past a doubt:—
> And now, ye learned, point that Nature out.
> To *follow Nature is* the path to truth;—
> But who's to find it? Unexperienc'd youth?
> The thought's ridiculous; yet youth's the time,
> When *Nature's talents* are the most in prime.—
> But *Nature's Knowledge* is another thing:—
> Few study music—yet how many sing?

10 *A Letter to David Garrick, Esq.* (1772), pp. 30–1.
11 George Alexander Stevens, *The Adventures of a Speculist* (1788), ii. 131.

Few study Nature—yet how many play,
And strut, and rant and whine three hours away?
Few *study* Nature; there are few who can;—
To study Nature is to study Man.
Man, too, must here be studied in the whole,
The human *body*, and the human *soul*.
Here, then, is *Nature*; here's the wanted fact;
How soul and body on each other act . . . [12]

Another answer is to be found in Garrick's own words[13] about performing one of his most famous comic roles, Abel Drugger, the tobacconist in Ben Jonson's *The Alchemist*:

When *Abel Drugger* has broke the Urinal, he is *mentally absorb'd* with the different Ideas of the *invaluable* Price of the Urinal . . . [This is] the Situation of his Mind. How are the different Members of the Body to be agitated? Why this,—His *Eyes* must be revers'd from the Object he is most intimidated with, and by dropping his *Lip* at the same time *to* the Object, it throws a trembling *Languor* upon every *Muscle*, and by declining the right Part of the Head *towards* the *Urinal*, it casts the most comic Terror and Shame over all the *upper* Part of the Body, that can be imagin'd . . . he will unavoidably give himself a Tremor in the *knees*, and if his Fingers, at the same time, seem *convuls'd*, it finishes the compleatest low Picture of *Grotesque Terror* that can be imagin'd by a *Dutch* Painter.

The setting of eyes, lip, head, knees made up an 'attitude' that laid bare Drugger's character and illuminated any words that he spoke. Eyes, voice and limbs were to be equally revealing in Garrick's description of Macbeth's stance when Duncan is murdered:

[Macbeth should be] a *moving Statue*, or indeed a *petrify'd Man;* his Eyes must Speak, and his Tongue be metaphorically silent; his Ears must be sensible of imaginary Noises, and *deaf* to the present and *audible* Voice of his Wife; his Attitudes must be *quick and permanent*; his Voice *articulately trembling*, and confusedly intelligible; the Murderer should be seen in *every Limb*.

---

12 *Chester Chronicle*, 20 November 1775; ascribed to 'the late Mr. Giffard.'
13 *An Essay on Acting* (1744), pp. 6–9.

In comedy or tragedy stance was highly significant, reinforcing speech and sometimes supplying it with meaning. The look in the eyes, movement in the lip or inclination of the head were also a necessary part of what Cibber had derisively called Garrick's 'pantomimical manner of acting', because miming was its foundation.

Samuel Johnson said to Mrs. Thrale, 'David, Madam, looks much older than he is, because his face has had double the business of any other man's. It is never at rest.' When the great actor wished to entertain his friends, he stood behind a chair and merely by the movement of his face conveyed every sort of passion, blending one into the other at will.[14] He was fortunate in his physical equipment: his features were strong and the bone structure was well suited to artificial lighting. His eyes were large with dark, expressive pupils. His head and arm movements were neat yet powerful, exceptionally quick but astonishingly graceful. His meaning was plain without the use of words, as is apparent in the following report: 'A young gentleman (deaf and dumb from his birth) having been at Drury Lane Theatre on Monday last to see Mr. Garrick perform the part of Hamlet was questioned as to his opinion of the performance, upon which he wrote the following lines:

> When Britain's Roscius on the Stage appears,
> Who charms all eyes, and (I am told) all ears;
> With ease the various passions I can trace
> Clearly reflected from *his* wondrous face;
> Whilst true conception with just action join'd,
> Strongly impress each image on my mind:
> —What need of *sounds*? when plainly I descry
> Th'expressive FEATURES, and the *speaking* EYE;
> That Eye, whose bright and penetrating ray,
> Does *Shakespear's* meaning to my soul convey.—
> Best Commentator on Great SHAKESPEAR's text!
> When GARRICK acts, no passage seems perplext.'[15]

14 Charles Dibdin, *History of the Stage*, v. 103.
15 *London Chronicle*, 2–4 January 1772. The young deaf gentleman may have had help in writing this.

A German visitor noted that he had 'the slightest muscle of his body and especially of his face under such control that he can represent all the emotions of the soul so that others may see them plainly.'[16] His 'eye' was especially praised. One critic wrote, 'his lively and piercing Eyes, are particularly happy in the Expression of sudden Joy or quick Rage.'[17] Tate Wilkinson put the more general outlook when he said, 'Garrick certainly possessed most extraordinary powers of eye, as they contained not only the fire and austerity he meant to convey, but his simplicity as Scrub, and archness of eye in Don John, was equally excellent and as various.'[18]

The same German visitor noted that Garrick's voice came over very distinctly in the playhouse, and we know from other sources that his stage whisper was piercing. To his excellent talents as a mimic, he added a voice that was a most flexible instrument and a technique of pointing verse in a most dramatic way. Theophilus Cibber wrote scornfully, as we have seen, of Garrick's 'unnatural Pauses in the middle of a Sentence,' but in these matters one would rather trust Garrick's sense of stagecraft than Cibber's. If he paused in the middle of a sentence, it was to emphasise what followed and to bring in a subtlety that had escaped the Cibbers of this world. He knew that an arrested movement of the body or the voice rivets an audience's attention.[19]

In spite of the critics I have quoted, Garrick's performances in certain Shakespearean characters were thought the finest ever known. A brief examination of some of them will indicate where his greatness lay.

His skill in miming for tragic effect is best seen in the ghost's entrance in the opening scene of *Hamlet*. G. C. Lichtenberg thought Garrick looked transfixed, his arms stretched high,

16 J. A. Kelly, *German Visitors to English Theaters in the Eighteenth Century* (Princeton, 1936), p. 65.
17 *A Treatise on the Passions*, p. 15.
18 *Memoirs* (York, 1790), iv. 42.
19 See *The Letters of David Garrick* (ed. Little and Kahrl, Cambridge, Mass., 1963), p. 350, where Garrick defends his own practice.

knees giving, legs apart, an expression of terror on his face. Lichtenberg himself felt quite distraught before the player had breathed the words, 'Angels and ministers of grace defend us.' The audience too was terrified by the look Hamlet gave Horatio and Marcellus when they tried to hold him back. With his sword before him, Garrick crept after the ghost and, moving and breathing heavily, was lost to sight.[20] His consternation when the ghost entered in the closet scene, was marked by Hamlet's kicking down the chair, a piece of stage business well timed and greatly appreciated.[21]

Garrick's miming was also seen to great tragic advantage in *Macbeth*. Thomas Davies tells us how he rejoined Lady Macbeth after the murder of Duncan:

The representation of this terrible part of the play, by Garrick and Mrs. Pritchard, can no more be described than I believe it can be equalled. I will not separate these performers, for the merits of both were transcendent. His distraction of mind and agonizing horrors were finely contrasted by her seeming apathy, tranquillity, and confidence. The beginning of the scene after the murder was conducted in terrifying whispers. Their looks and action supplied the place of words. You heard what they spoke, but you learned more from the agitation of mind displayed in their action and deportment. The poet here gives only an outline to the consummate actor.—*I have done the deed!—Didst thou not hear a noise?—When?—* *—Did you not speak?*—The dark colouring, given by the actor to these abrupt speeches, makes the scene awful and tremendous to the auditors. The wonderful expression of heartful horror, which Garrick felt when he shewed his bloody hands, can only be conceived and described by those who saw him.[22]

A foreigner, who knew no English, was so upset by the scene that he fainted away.[23]

20 See *Lichtenberg's Visits to England* (Translated and annotated by M. L. Mare and W. H. Quarrell, Oxford, 1938), pp. 7–10.
21 [J. Hill] *The Actor* (1755), p. 276.
22 *Dramatic Miscellanies* (Dublin, 1784), ii. 93–4.
23 W. D. Robson-Scott, *German Travellers in England*, 1400–1800 (Oxford, 1953), p. 144.

References to Garrick's performance of Lear concern themselves more with his speaking of the verse and particularly of his denunciation of his daughters. The most interesting of them lays stress upon the variety of effects that Garrick achieved in what was, of course, the Nahum Tate version of *King Lear*;

You fall precipitately upon your knees, extend your Arms—clench your Hands—set your Teeth—And with a savage Distraction in your Look—trembling in all your Limbs—and your Eyes pointed to Heaven, (the whole expressing a fulness of Rage and Revenge) you begin
Hear Nature, Dear Goddess!—
with a *broken, inward, eager* Utterance; from thence rising every Line in Loudness and Rapidity of Voice till you come to
and feel
How sharper than a Serpent's Tooth it is,
To have a thankless Child.
Then you are struck at once with your Daughter's Ingratitude, and bursting into Tears, with a most sorrowful Heart-breaking Tone of voice, you say
—go, go, my People.
This in my Opinion is the strongest Climax of Rage; and the break from it at the end of the Speech, gives a natural necessary Variety, and was visibly design'd so by the Author . . . [24]

The critic was not so impressed by Garrick's reaction to the curse: 'When you burst into Tears at the End of the Curse, you need not make use of your Handkerchief; your Change of Voice sufficiently marks your Distress; and your Application to your Handkerchief is, perhaps, too minute a Circumstance, and makes you more present to Things, than you ought to be at that Time.'[25] In another book the same observer was more damning, and wrote of Garrick's 'unmanly snivelling . . . like a vex'd girl', but had to concede that the great actor was 'successful in tincturing all the Passions, with a certain Feebleness suitable to the Age of the King.'[26]

[24] *An Examen into a New Comedy call'd The Suspicious Husband* (1747), p. 31.
[25] *Ibid.*, p. 37.
[26] [S. Foote] *A Treatise on the Passions (c.* 1747), pp. 17, 19.

Anti-climax was always possible in such a contrast between majestic grief and a childishness close to senility. The handkerchief might appear too trivial in a display of the King's overwhelming sorrow, yet its use could be defended on the ground that it was so ordinary and commonplace that it became a symbol of great weakness, bringing the audience into closer touch with him.

The author of *A Letter of Compliment to the Ingenious Author of a Treatise on the Passions* attempted a more elaborate defence of Garrick's interpretation of the part: 'When *Lear*, after having given Way to several Bursts of Indignation, and running from one dismal Reflection to another, is torn to Pieces with the extremity of his Disappointment and Distress, and prepares on his knees, a solemn Invocation of an imaginary Deity to revenge in a terrible Manner his inhuman Wrongs—that then I say, the *Violence* and *Force* of his Passion, must of necessity *be Curbs to his natural Powers, his Voice low and solemn*, but forcible *and earnest*, his Utterance slow and deliberate, and, no doubt, an extravagant *Wildness in the Eyes*. In this Light the greatest Actor that ever trod the *English* stage . . . considers this Passage; and throughout the whole Speech conveys such sweet Pain to his Hearers.'[27]

To the objections that Garrick ought not to have sat on the joint-stool with Edgar or picked straws, the writer of *A Letter of Compliment* replies, 'This pretty Critick, I am apt to think, has never yet seen Bedlam . . . the Words and Actions of a Madman have seldom any kind of Connection whatsoever. It is a common Thing to observe these unhappy People, while they are learnedly entertaining you with Discourses of the highest Importance and Weight; at the same Instant employ'd in Actions of the most frivolous Nature.' The argument is one that Garrick would have supported because it was his habit to base his interpretations on a close scrutiny of particular people in particular circumstances. When he had been working up the part of Lear, he had studied the behaviour of an acquaintance,

[27] P. 20.

who had gone mad after killing his young daughter by accidentally letting her fall from a height.[28] Garrick turned his observations to good professional use.

He showed equal care in his performances as Richard III, and Theophilus Cibber alone ridiculed the way in which Garrick began his interpretation: 'For the sake of an Attitude, which is sure to be dwelt on 'till the Audience clap,—this Sentence ["And descant on my own Deformity"] is commonly clos'd with an Action of pointing to the Ground, and fixing the Eye thereon for some Time, as if Richard had a real delight in ruminating on his uncouth Person.'[29] A writer in the *Theatrical Review*, however, pointed out that this was one of the very few soliloquies that Garrick spoke to the audience, and that he usually delivered them 'walking to and fro, without looking [at] or minding the spectators, who are not supposed to be present.'[30] Again Garrick must be counted wiser than Cibber: his reason for differentiating in this way was surely that Richard was not someone thinking aloud to put his ideas in order, but one who was amusing himself and the audience with an ironical justification of his own outlook.

His acting in the 'tent-scene' at the end of the play was greatly admired for its timing and general control. Roger Pickering commented on the moment when 'that Monster in Blood and excessive Villa[i]ny wakes in all the Terrors of an Imagination distracted by conscious Guilt:

> *Richard.* Give me a Horse—bind up my Wounds!
> Have mercy, Heav'n!

What *masterly Expression* has the great Shakespeare shewn in these eleven Words! The rapid Incoherence of the first Line, presents strongly to us the guilty confusion of Richard's Senses, scarce yet awake, at the Eve of Battle, which might bring him a full Punishment for his enormous Crimes; and, for the first

28 A. Murphy, *The Life of David Garrick* (1801), i. 30.
29 *Two Dissertations on the Theatres* (1756), p. 65.
30 (1758), p. 11.

Time, forces him to address that Heaven which, he believed, he had offended beyond *Forgiveness* . . . But, to bring a remorseless Wretch to *Feeling*, and from *Feeling* to *Pray*, requires a Pause indeed. Exquisitely just and beautiful is Shakespeare's *Expression*; exquisitely just and beautiful is Garrick's *Action*, in so small a Compass.'[31]

In one of the last performances he gave before retiring, Garrick reverted to this role: 'He played the part very differently from the manner in which the character has of late been given to the public. It was no longer the raving madman who bullied all about him. In the first act the calm subtlety of the poet was admirably expressed. In the scene with Lady Anne, nothing could exceed the fine deceptive style of his address . . . In the fifth act the full force of his voice was exerted, and the spirit of the character maintained with the strictest propriety.'[32]

The *Theatrical Examiner*[33] noted that he had 'a quick and amazing art of magnifying trifles, which is sometimes the force of trick: not always taste and nature'. Yet at its best this art gave an audience great insight into character, and had always been more usually employed in comedy than tragedy. In fact, I think it might be argued that Garrick brought back to tragedy some effects deliberately excluded by tragedians who aimed above all at stateliness.

The same critic noted that the new methods might well tend to a loss of dignity in comedy, too, and remarked: 'a man who would have his deportment lively with elegance, must vastly avoid the air of a squirt. When he [Garrick] plays Archer, he makes me forget the intention of the author so greatly, that I have lost the gentleman in disguise.'[34] The same school of thought found that all Garrick's deficiencies of dignity and power were caused by the fact that he was only sixty-four inches tall. There was little justification for the complaint: short stature is much less of a liability on the stage than great height,

31 *Reflections upon Theatrical Expression in Tragedy* (1755), p. 50.
32 *Chester Chronicle*, 6 June 1776.
33 (1757), p. 32.   34 *Ibid.*, p. 26.

and Garrick was able to off-set any disadvantages by the wonderful fluency of his physical responses. In fact, Lichtenberg said, 'there is in Mr. Garrick's whole figure, movements, and propriety of demeanour something which I have met with rarely in a few Frenchmen I have seen and never, except in this instance, among the large number of Englishmen with whom I am acquainted . . . It is therefore refreshing to see his manner of walking, shrugging his shoulders, putting his hands into his pockets, putting on his hat, now pulling it down over his eyes.'[35] These movements were full of character, and were a delight to watch for themselves alone. It may be that they were so popular that he overdid them:

> His over frequent turning round about,
> His handkerchief for ever in and out,
> His hat still moulded in a thousand forms,
> His pocket clapping when his passion storms.[36]

The mannerisms may have irritated the perfectionist, but they can be properly seen as showing an excess of nervous energy.

Garrick's greatness as a tragic actor was undoubtedly equalled, if not surpassed, by his skill in comedy. Miming, again, was the basis of his achievements. Consider the following description of the harassed Sir John Brute returning home: 'Whoever has seen him [Garrick] sit down in his Chair, must acknowledge that Sleep comes upon him by the most natural Gradations: Not the minutest Circumstance about a Man in that Situation escapes him: The Struggle between Sleep and his Unwillingness to give way to it is perfectly just: The Lid depressed, yet faintly raised; the Change of his Voice from distinct Articulation to a confused Murmuring: The sudden Oppression of his Senses and the Recovery from it; his then beginning again his broken Chain of Thoughts, and the malicious Smile that unexpectedly gleams from him, till he is at length totally overpowered, are all such acknowledged Strokes

---

[35] *Lichtenberg's Visits to England* (Translated and Annotated by M. L. Mare and W. H. Quarrell, Oxford, 1938), p. 6.

[36] F.B.L., *The Rational Rosciad* (1767), p. 17.

C

of Art, that they keep the whole House agitated at once with Laughter, and Admiration.'[37]

As Abel Drugger, too, he greatly impressed the audience by showing the gullible tobacconist touchingly delighted to find his name of all names to be the one spelled out from the stars, but keeping his exultation to himself and from the too-knowing world. This was all done without exaggeration: 'there is no

THE LONDON THEATRES. *PLATE II.* *Engraved for the Universal Museum.*

Mr. Garrick in the Character of Abel Drugger in the Alchymist. Act IV. Scene IV.
Published according to Act of Parliament by J. Payne in Pater Noster Row.

twisting of Features, no Squinting, but all is correct as if a real Tobacco Boy were before us. It is really surprising how he [Garrick], who has occasionally looked unutterable Things, can present us with such a Face of Inanity.'[38]

His range of comic characterisation was considerable. He was thought brilliant as Benedick, particularly in the rallies of wit. He delighted in the role of Ranger, the gallant in Hoadly's

37 *London Chronicle*, 1–3 March 1757.
38 *Ibid.*, 5–8 March 1757.

The Suspicious Husband, and so great was his personal charm that a contemporary remarked, 'he was by nature formed to please the sex; and I believe there was scarce a woman off or on the stage, who saw him in Ranger, that did not wish to be Mrs. Strictland.'[39] As the foppish Fribble in his own *Miss in Her Teens,* he filled Covent Garden. Don John (in *The Chances*) was in his hands 'a new created personage'.[40] In Frances Sheridan's *The Discovery* (1763), he played the formal old bachelor so drolly that he kept the audience 'in a continued roar of laughter.'[41] As he himself had said, the only way to become excellent at portraying 'characters of humour' was by getting to know human nature. They only became alive, however, when he brought to bear on them all the resources of his superb technique.

Garrick's superiority over the ordinary actors of his day was often mentioned. His art was full of subtle variety; they were said to 'gesticulate incessantly with their hands like theological students in a pulpit, and scan their lines till one's ears ache.'[42] Of all the players in both theatres, he was the only one who knew how to stand still.[43] He usually ignored the audience when he soliloquised, but Yates addressed it so directly 'as to throw the upper part of his body over the orchestra.'[44] Once when he acted Richard III, his Richmond was Palmer, who 'appeared to have lost his own guts and to exhibit nothing but a lank, callicoe carcase stuffed with wind.'[45] Yet 'when *Macbeth* sees the *horrid Shadow* of his murder'd Friend, seated at a Banquet . . . I have observed the Refuse of the Theatre, *Macbeth's* Company, Creatures who seldom betray any Idea of Nature or Feeling, behave in the justest Manner in this Scene, merely

---

39 *A Dialogue in the Shades between the celebrated Mrs. Cibber and the no less celebrated Mrs. Woffington* (1766), p. 4.
40 *London Chronicle,* 25–26 January 1757.
41 *Ibid.,* 3–5 February 1763.
42 J. A. Kelly, *German Visitors to English Theaters* (Princeton, 1936), p. 37.
43 *London Chronicle,* 3–5 October 1758.
44 *The Theatrical Review* (1758), p. 11.
45 *Morning Chronicle,* 6 June 1776.

from the Infection they have caught from the Countenance of their Roscius.'[46]

The strongest distinction between them was made by the quarrelsome critic, George Steevens, who had been present at a performance of Aaron Hill's *Zara*: 'I think you never played Lusignan so happily as on Saturday night; at least you never affected me in it, so much before.—But what shall I say of your other performers? Are there words to be found that can convey any adequate idea of their incomparable badness? Had I been a cannibal, I think I could scarce have ventured to sup upon them so surely should I have been sick with gorging such cats'-meat and dogs'-meat. Have you no better stuff behind the scenes? or can you be so mistaken as to suppose you need these wretched foils to shew you off to advantage? Whether Miss Sherry, Miss Young, Mr. Brereton, Mr. Reddish or Mr. Aickin, was the most contemptible I really think no unprejudiced Spectator could honestly determine. Even sentiment itself had no effect, but could scarce procure a feeble clap from our hard-handed friends above stairs. To say the truth, I never saw such a miserable pack of Strollers in quiet possession of a Theatre Royal. . . . The play was so cut, that though we stay'd it out we were here at supper by half an hour after nine. Every line not absolutely necessary to the action seem'd to be omitted. . . . If on saturday night you had not afforded the public a transient glimpse of yourself, you would not have had money enough in the house to pay for candles.—I think, in a future Season, if you have no better actors, we may fairly excuse you from the expence of wax, you only granting us in our turn the ancient privileges of Sadler's Wells—viz. a free use of pipes, porter and Shrimps. Heaven preserve you! and keep me from ever seeing more of Zara than the second act!'[47] We are forced to discount some of Steevens' more sweeping statements

---

[46] *A Letter of Compliment to the Ingenious Author of a Treatise on the Passions*, p. 15.

[47] Folger Shakespeare Library MS. Box 55: Steevens, 1185, dated Jany. 2nd. 1775.

because they suggest he had a spiteful rather than a judicial temper but even when this allowance is made, we cannot find much merit in the cast.

There were leading players, however, who were really respected for their professional attainments. Garrick outdid them all in his versatility and depth of imagination, but some of them surpassed him in particular roles.

Spranger Barry was a more accomplished performer of Othello and Lord Townly. His superb build gave him a most dignified bearing, and his voice was perfectly suited to the Moor because it was 'between the treble and the base, rather hollow and deep . . . , very fit for the utterance of the inward notes of tender pangs, stifled, struggling.'[48] It was also very clear and distinct, and enabled him to make transitions from elation to despair in a way that gave audiences enormous pleasure. In an effort to convey the scalp-tingling quality of Barry's voice, Paul Hiffernan compared it with the peculiar bark of hounds at the sight of game: 'In deep Distress, he has a Heart-searching Break in his Voice, even to a Melody; and not unlike the Murmuring of the Wood quest.'[49] His Face, too, suggested consuming jealousy: 'When Othello says

> Had all his hairs been lives
> My great revenge had stomach for them all,

we see Mr. Barry redden thro' the very black of his face; his whole visage becomes inflamed; his eyes sparkle with successful vengeance, and he seems to raise himself above the ground while he pronounces it.'[50] It is curious that Barry should have been able to convey this impression when Garrick failed to do so. The muscles of Garrick's face, it had been noted, 'follow with the most minute propriety the impression of his soul',[51] but in his particular case "the blacking screens, and renders in-

---

48 *The Theatrical Review*, p. 23.
49 *The Tuner* (1756), p. 18
50 [John Hill] *The Actor* (1755), p. 9.
51 *The Theatrical Review*, p. 2.

communicable to spectators, all impassioned working of the countenance.'[52]

Barry's contest with Garrick, when each played the part of Romeo at the rival houses for twelve consecutive nights in 1751, drew the well-known comment:

'Well, what's tonight?' says angry Ned,
As up from bed he rouses:
'Romeo again!' and shakes his head—
Ah, *Pox on both your houses!*'[53]

Barry was said to excel in the first three acts, and Garrick in the last two. Mrs. Pritchard declared that Garrick's passion was so fiery that she expected to see him come climbing up to the balcony, but Barry's voice was so winning she knew she would have gone down to greet him.[54] Both of them adopted the famous 'attitude' in which Romeo raised the iron to dash out Paris's brains, so both were criticised for lack of truth to character: 'Vastly as this attitude is applauded, it is false. The weapon of a gentleman is his sword, he naturally has recourse to it, and no other.'[55]

Barry was a noble Antony and a tender Lear. His movements seemed more suited to a Roman 'shape' than to eighteenth-century costume, and his tongue preferred Shakespearean blank verse to everyday speech. An interesting summary of his characteristics was provided by the malicious 'Sir Nicholas Nipclose' (Francis Gentleman):

With voice harmonious, yet too apt to whine
Music of sound his principal design;
Measure of verse not sense bespoke his care
And rants were catch'd at, to make groundlings stare.
Without variety of action, still
His arms and legs obeyed *mechanic* will;
Yet, with all faults, none more could flood each eye,
None better form'd to make the ladies sigh.[56]

52 Paul Hiffernan, *Dramatic Genius* (1772), p. 18.
53 *Daily Advertiser*, 1 October 1750.
54 P. Fitzgerald, *Life of D. Garrick*, i. 257.
55 [John Hill] *The Actor*, p. 283.   56 *The Theatres* (1772), p. 44.

It is not surprising to find that his talent lay in tragedy, and that in comedy he was usually mediocre.

Barry had learned much from Garrick, and their differences in style were caused more by their physical characteristics and imaginative capacity than by contrasted conventions of playing. In James Quin, however, Garrick had a rival who belonged to the older school of acting, one that was nicely described by Richard Cumberland: 'Quin presented himself upon the rising of the curtain [as Horatio in Rowe's *The Fair Penitent*] in a green velvet coat embroidered down the seams, an enormous full-bottomed periwig, rolled stockings and high-heeled square-toed shoes: with a very little variation of cadence, and in a deep full tone, accompanied by a sawing kind of action, which had more of the senate than of the stage in it, he rolled out his heroics with an air of dignified indifference, that seemed to disdain the plaudits that were bestowed upon him. Mrs. Cibber [as Calista] in a key, high-pitched but sweet withal, sung or rather recitatived Rowe's harmonious strain . . . : it was so wanting in contrast, that, though it did not wound the ear, it wearied it.'[57] Then Garrick came on as Lothario, 'alive in every muscle, and in every feature . . . it seemed as if a whole century had been stept over in the transition of a single scene.' But the audiences of 1746, listening to 'the dialogue of alter- cation between Horatio and Lothario bestowed far the greater *show of hands* upon the master of the old school than upon the founder of the new.'[58] Time was needed to effect the change from the old conventions, but it is always important to remem- ber that the old methods still moved an audience accustomed to them. They appeared stilted and artificial only to the new generation of playgoers. In due course their successors would delight in the formal, and further away again there would be another return to naturalism. Any convention is acceptable if we are used to it, and we must not make the mistake of under- rating Quin's talents just because he was overtaken by fashion. In an engraving that shows him as Coriolanus, he looks ludi-

[57] *Memoirs* (1807), i. 80–1.   [58] *Ibid.*, i. 82.   31

crous in his stiff skirt, peruke, and plume, and Charles Churchill
had no difficulty in ridiculing him in four lines of *The Rosciad*:

> His eyes, in gloomy socket taught to roll,
> Proclaim'd the sullen habit of his soul,
> Heavy and phlegmatic he trod the stage
> Too proud for Tenderness, to dull for Rage.

Sir Charles Hanbury-Williams's epigram on him commented
severely on his 'peculiar absurdities' as well as his 'plumb-
pudding' face, and ended:

> He felt as he spoke, Nature's dictates are true,
> When he acted the part, his own picture he drew.[59]

Yet he had a strong pleasant voice and could declaim well in
parts like Cato or Brutus, as well as in the English version of
Racine's *Andromaque*, Ambrose Philips's *The Distrest Mother*.
If he could not cope with swift changes of emotion, he spoke
'sentiments' with authority and was a notable Pierre in Otway's
Venice Preserved. His sonority of utterance made him an impres-
sive Ghost in *Hamlet*, and Duke in *Measure for Measure*. 'Mr.
Quin possessed the tone of majesty, and till somebody else can
say, "Porcia is dead", as we have heard him chill an audience
by pronouncing it, we must allow that excellence lost to us.'[60]
At the other extreme, his own very personal sense of humour
gave comic penetration to his portrayals of Heartwell (in *The
Old Bachelor*), Apemantus, Sullen (in *The Beaux' Stratagem*),
Ballance (in *The Recruiting Officer*), Manly and Maskwell. His
Falstaff was acknowledged to be a delightful impersonation,
and his Sir John Brute, as amusing as Garrick's.

Another actor who clung to the old tradition and was most
impressive in declamation was Thomas Sheridan. A thoughtful
man of good education, he applied his mind to elocution and
was much admired by those who disliked Garrick's 'tricks and
bo-peeps'. The *Theatrical Examiner*, for example, said Hamlet

---

59   *The Works of the Right Honourable Sir Charles Hanbury-Williams, K.B.*,
     (1822), ii. 270.
60   *The Actor*, p. 205.

was a character often attempted 'but never tolerably by any but Sheridan'. It also praised his Macbeth, finding him very good in the dagger scene,[61] but another critic wrote of the same performance, 'Then the cold Sheridan half froze the part.'[62] Like Quin, he could be very fine in roles like Cato and Brutus, in which loftiness of sentiment and integrity of character were everything. Even as King John he was much admired, and his son, Richard Brinsley Sheridan, said that 'his scene with Hubert was a master-piece of the art; and no actor could ever reach its excellence.'[63] He wrote frequently on elocution but it is difficult to discover how far his theories affected his artistic practice. What is clear from the following example is that he had studied the subject minutely:

In the following lines of Shakespeare

> The raven himself's not hoarse
> That croaks the fatal entrance of Duncan
> Under these battlements—

The sound of the *r* is to be softened, Lady Macbeth, by these words, does not mean to convey an unpleasant idea.

The power of *f* when preceded by a short *u*, is often expressive of the idea; as in the words bluff, gruff, rough, tough, rebuff, etc., and in these cases its sound may be continued. It should also be forcibly pronounced, whenever expression demands it. As

> —mild was he with the mild,
> But with the froward he was fierce as fire.[64]

Sheridan had an original mind, but seems to have been more interested in words and sounds than in character and action.

At the other extreme from Sheridan and Quin stood Charles Macklin. Like them, he understood the importance of good diction, but he aimed at a natural rather than a mannered style, as is shown in his description of his first London performance: 'I spoke so familiar, sir, and so little in the *hoity-toity*

---

61 Pp. 25, 29, 81.
62 *London Chronicle*, 28–30 October 1773.
63 Michael Kelly, *Reminiscences* (2nd ed., 1826), ii. 315.
64 *Lectures on the Art of Reading* (2nd ed., 1781), p. 65.

tone of the tragedy of that day, that the Manager told me I had better go to grass for another year or two.' A former friend of Garrick, he shared (and may even have influenced) the great actor's outlook, disciplining himself and all around him in the great aim of revealing human nature with fidelity. His range was confined, but he stamped his idiosyncratic personality on two characters in his own plays, Sir Archy MacSarcasm in *Love à la Mode* and Sir Pertinax MacSycophant in *The Man of the World*. His hooked nose and slit mouth gave him a villainous appearance, and he made the most of it when he played Shylock. For him the usurer was no figure of fun but a bitter man reacting fiercely against the scornful treatment he had received from the Venetians. Macklin wore a red 'piqued beard' and loose, black gown, and gave local colour to the production by donning the red hat of the jews of Venice. In the third act, he reported: 'I threw out all my fire, and as the contrasted passions of joy for the Merchant's losses, and grief for the elopment of Jessica, opened a fine field for the actor's powers, I had the good fortune to please beyond my warmest expecta-tions.'[65] In the trial scene his miming was so powerful that when he came to sharpen his knife on the floor, he sent a shudder through the audience. His performances as Iago were also famous, but here his features rather handicapped him. As one critic said, 'M——— has such a strong Stamp of the Villain imprinted on his Countenance . . . that we can't help thinking it a weakness in *Othello* to have any Concern with him at all.'[66] But he thought all such critics fools and knaves, and in a spirit of complete independence gave himself up to a system of acting that avoided ranting, starts, and attitudes, for the communication of great depth of feeling by emphatic gesture and telling looks.

His pupil, Samuel Foote, possessed much of his sharpness and little of his intensity. Foote's medium was satirical farce, and his aim the cruel exaggeration of personal foibles by witty

[65] W. Cooke, *Memoirs of Charles Macklin* (1804), pp. 92–4.
[66] *A Letter of Compliment*, p. 27.

mimicry. D'Archenholz watched him closely and said, 'He knew how to imitate with great exactness the gait and conversation of any one, and never forgot to place his hero in the most foolish and ridiculous point of view. When he played, the house, during the whole representation, was affected with a continual and convulsive laughter.'[67] In some of his plays (like *The Maid of Bath*) the objects of his satire well deserved ridicule and Foote took over the function of the public castigator; in others (like *The Minor*) his personal spleen was too obvious to be anything but a display of smart ferocity. When the effervescent Boswell said that Foote had a singular talent of exhibiting characters, Samuel Johnson properly rebuked him: 'Sir, it is not a talent; it is a vice; it is what others abstain from. It is not comedy, which exhibits the character of a species, as that of a miser gathered from many misers: it is farce, which exhibits individuals.'[68] O'Keeffe excused what appears to be Foote's malignity by saying that he had to surround himself by people who would laugh at his jokes, but this surely implies that they would laugh only at malice. O'Keeffe also added, 'He had a wink, and a smile with one corner of his mouth, a harsh voice, except when mimicking. His manner on the stage was not very pleasant to the performers on with him, for he tried to engross all the attention.'[69] Foote's renown was derived entirely from his spirited but mocking imitations. One of the few parts (outside his own farces) that he won any praise in, was Sir Paul Plyant in Congreve's *The Double Dealer*.[70]

Two other comic actors were very popular in the theatres of the period. Thomas Weston was a small man with a 'wooden' expression, but when he spoke with characteristic slowness in his flat voice, he had the audience helpless with mirth. Lichtenberg has left a memorable discription of how Weston and Garrick played up to each other as Scrub and Archer in

67 *A Picture of England* (Dublin, 1791), p. 240.
68 Boswell's Life of Johnson (ed. G. B. Hill and L. F. Powell, Oxford, 1934), ii. 95.
69 J. O'Keeffe, *Recollections* (1826), i. 328–9.
70 *The Theatrical Examiner* (1757), p. 47.

The Beaux' Stratagem. Scrub was anxious, in his artless simplicity, to reach the high standards of the man about town, and pitiably tried to imitate Archer's method of crossing his legs and smoothing his stockings. On another occasion, the German visitor recalled seeing him in a play 'where a pretty chambermaid stroked his cheeks in order to influence him in the cause of her mistress. His face lighted up very slowly, but finally to such a degree that at least two dozen teeth, many of which were of no small proportion, appeared; there was scarce a mouth in the house which did not, each in his own manner, laugh or smile in sympathy.'[71] This ability to draw out warm feeling is almost as important in the comedian's equipment as his remarkable sense of timing: Weston was loved and admired. In his own way he even surpassed David Garrick as Abel Drugger.

Shuter was another comedian who enjoyed considerable popularity in his day, but unlike Weston, he seems to have been guilty at times of overplaying. The *Theatrical Examiner* warned him about this: 'Be comic, Mr. S———r!—not too comical! you can make your face mighty droll: but twisting wry faces is not always just and humourous. Falstaff is a part of too much weight for Mr. S———r.' It damned him more effectively in the sentence, 'Mr. S———r can play little low parts that require no great weight,—with an agreeable spirit of humour that is very well.'[72] In fact he created the roles of Croaker in Goldsmith's *The Good Natured Man*, Hardcastle in *She Stoops to Conquer*, and Sir Anthony in *The Rivals*. His parts ranged from Ben in *Love for Love* to Mercutio and Teague, and he was much admired for his Stephen in *Every Man in his Humour* and Corbaccio in *Volpone*. A certain gusto marked them all.

Some players were pre-eminent in their 'walks', the types usually allotted to them. Yates played old men and had one curious advantage: 'his countenance in general, but more particularly his eyes, become the artificial wrinkles, and yet

71 'Lichtenberg's Letters concerning Garrick . . . ' (translated by J. F. Williams), *The Bibliographer*, ii (New York, 1903), 372.

72 P. 44.

have archness enough not to look amiss in the characters of valets, of fools in Shakespeare's plays, etc.'[73] Woodward was a famous Harlequin, but his peculiar drawl and manner allowed him to 'play some parts of Tinsel well,—Captain Bobadil, Flash, and the fine gentleman in *Lethe*, vastly well indeed.'[74] At the age of sixty, he created the role of the youthful Jack Absolute. Dodd was renowned as a fop, either comical or villainous:

> In Faddle Dodd with energy of art
> Joins the fop's figure to the villain's heart.

Baddeley specialised in foreign footmen, revealing 'their abjectness and pride.'[75]

The leading actresses of the day were equally skilful at their business. D'Archenholz thought they were much more adaptable than the men in translated plays like *Zara* and *Iphigenia*: 'the actresses support the honour of the theatres, by means of a nobleness and a dignity which charm the beholder.'[76] They were helped by the fact that their clothes were nearer the fashionable styles of the eighteenth century, and they never looked as odd as some of the leading actors.

Mrs. Pritchard's enunciation was highly praised as 'a vocal delivery ever varied and ever just', but her gestures were confined to wrist and fingers. Her mannerism, too, of tossing her head when wishing to suggest impatience or distress was thought inadequate.[77] Although she was undoubtedly among the greatest tragic actresses of the century, her style of playing did not please everyone: 'She is often truly natural and agreeable, yet have I seen her bring some scenes in tragedy down to a familiarity that was rather PETIT: for instance, Lady Macbeth, however just and well she may be in most parts of it, is yet tinctured with this failing. In Zara, when she finds Osmyn

73 *The Theatrical Review* (1758), p. 11.
74 *The Theatrical Examiner* (1757), p. 42.
75 *Anti-Thespis* (1767), pp. 11–12.
76 *A Picture of London*, p. 239.
77 *The Theatrical Review*, pp. 16–17.

in the prison consoled by Almeria, she greatly wants a dignity in her anger: the best proof I can give her of it is, the laughter raised by the method of executing her part of the scene.' But she was excellent, the critic admitted, in Meropé, Beatrice, and Clarinda. Her brilliance in comedy was generally accepted. The same critic concluded, 'a little further dash of elegance would have made her nearer to an universal performer than any man or woman on the stage.'[78]

If Mrs. Pritchard came nearer the range and 'natural' style of Garrick than any other actress, Mrs. Cibber belonged to the older, more limited, school, and almost confined herself to tragedy. John Hill said that the 'naturally plaintive voice and melancholy tone' that qualified her 'so happily for some parts', made her 'less natural' in others.[79] This can be easily understood when we recollect the way in which she 'recitatived' Rowe's lines in *The Fair Penitent*, since the technique was well suited to the 'She-tragedies' of Rowe but not so appropriate for more robust characters. Wilkinson thought her cast of parts, Alicia, Constance, Ophelia, Indiana, Juliet was 'truly her own', and admired her elegance and neatness as Monimia.[80] David Williams said she 'was nature. She felt the passions in the highest degree; they tuned her voice and shaped her countenance.'[81] *The Theatrical Review* declared that 'Nature had bestowed on her an agreeable figure, a bewitching voice, and, above all, an exquisite feeling ... Could she but add to these charms a more majestic gait, and a little variety in her tones, my notions of tragedy-acting could not reach beyond her.' The same writer praised her easy carriage, but allowed that some people thought her action was 'not rich in descriptive gestures'.[82] A hostile critic remarked that her 'lifting up and down of the Arms, at almost every Period', was as tiresome as 'a continual, unpleasing Sameness in every Character she

[78] *The Theatrical Examiner*, pp. 49–50.
[79] *The Actor*, p. 60.
[80] *Memoirs*, iv. 164, 81.
[81] *A Letter to David Garrick, Esq.*, (1772), pp. 16–17.   [82] P. 15.

attempts.'[83] Foote, too, wished she would not shake her head quite so much, and put her hands together so often.[84] There seems to have been some monotony in her playing, but at her best she must have been most moving.

Mrs. Yates was another tragic actress who made a profound impression, but did not escape heavy criticism. Lichtenberg believed that she was 'so skilled in the management of her arms that from that woman alone could be made an abstract of the art of gesticulation.' Her figure was rather unwieldy, and she 'tot[t]er'd about to[o] much and flump'd down to[o] often' as entirely to disconcert her fellow-player, Mrs. Clive.[85] Mrs. Yates's qualities were summarised in *The Rational Rosciad*:

> Person she has, a voice distinct and clear,
> But harshness often grates upon the ear,
> Her hands and arms gymnastically thrown,
> A northern accent and a whining tone;
> Rowing and stooping, ever in address,
> Must make the pleasure to the audience less;
> Softness she wants in Belvidera's part,
> To gain the soul and steal into the heart.
> Virago's characters she's form'd to hit,
> But never with the sympathetic sit.[86]

An engraving of her as Calista in *The Fair Penitent* shows her in a stiff tragic 'attitude' with the dagger ready to be plunged into her bosom to the accompaniment of the words, 'It is but thus, and both are satisfied.'

The variety of rich characterisation that the English stage could offer at this period is also indicated in the talents of Peg Woffington. She could hold her own in tragedy, and was competent as Lady Macbeth, in *Jane Shore* or *Calista*. She even attempted the style of French classical tragedy: 'At her return from France she strove to introduce here many of the declamatory tones and laboured gestures, peculiar to that stage and

---

83 *A Letter of Compliment*, p. 35.
84 *The Roman and English Comedy Consider'd* (1747), p. 37.
85 Folger Library MS. Y. c. 552 (i).   86 P. 26.   39

ACTING

nation; but though very improper for our words, images and
feeling, they passed uncensured under the sanction of this loved
actress."[87] The same critic thought her 'the best lively coquette
that ever appeared on our stage, except Mrs. Oldfield.' She
radiated charm as Millamant in *The Way of the World* and Lady
Townly in *The Provoked Husband*. As one man remarked, 'She
first steals your Heart and then laughs at you as secure of your
Applause.' There was 'witchcraft in her Beauty' and she was
'superlatively engaging in genteel Comedy.'[88] She was also
renowned for her 'breeches' parts, delighting audiences with
her Sir Harry Wildair.

Another sprightly actress was Mrs. Clive. Dr. Johnson
thought her the best player he had ever watched, adding that
she was a better romp than he ever saw in nature. For Goldsmith
she had 'more true humour than any actor or actress upon the
English or any other stage I have seen.'[89] Her plain appearance
limited her to certain parts: 'the nimble Pertness of the
Chambermaid, who presumes upon the Favours of her Master;
the subtle Intrigues of *Flippanta*, the borrow'd Coquetry and
Affectation of *Mrs. Phillis*, the Good-Nature, Ignorance, and
aukward Surprize of *Nell Jobson*, and an innumerable train of
Characters of the same Stamp, establish their Value on the
Merit of her Representation.'[90] *The Theatrical Examiner* properly
warned her not to play the fine lady or tragedy heroine,[91] but
might have qualified this with a reference to her Lady Wishfor't:

Whilst with love's flame in hoary age she glows,
Vice in its full deformity she shews:
In fine, no player e'er possesst more art
To hit the real humour of each part.

Her technical resources are never described, but in comedy
they must have been much more than adequate.

Another who played coquettes admirably was Mrs. Abington.

87 *The Theatrical Review*, p. 37.   88 *A Letter of Compliment*, p. 34.
89 *Works* (ed. Friedman, Oxford, 1966), i. 451.
90 *A Letter of Compliment*, p. 33.   91 P. 53.

D'Archenholz judged her to be 'the greatest ornament of their stage, and [she] unites all parties in her praise. She attempts comedy alone, but with such a happy combination of nature and art, that I may affirm without fear, that so many talents were never united in any other female performer in Europe.'[92] She could play hoyden or fine lady equally well, and was noted for her performances as Miss Prue, Beatrice, and Lady Teazle. She was an intelligent woman who had learned to overcome her own deficiencies. Her voice was small and high-pitched, but she used it so perfectly as to be audible everywhere. Her career was, in every sense, a triumph of art.

Mrs. Bellamy, too, was intelligent, but owed her success far more to her beautiful face and figure. Her blue eyes dazzled young men and, when Garrick decided to compete with Barry, she was a very obvious choice as his Juliet. *The Theatrical Review* remarked[93] that in scenes of distress she had 'a soft wildness, which commands pity', adding 'her talents lie chiefly in the pathetic . . . she is not like most of the other actresses, reduced to the poor shift of hiding her face . . . real, undissembled tears then speak her feeling, and call forth fellow-drops from every eye'.

In his last season at Drury Lane, Garrick introduced into his company a provincial actress named Sarah Siddons. His friend Henry Bate had seen her at Cheltenham and had been struck by her 'propriety of diction as well as natural style of acting.'[94] She made no great impression in London and lost her post when R. B. Sheridan took over the management in June 1776. She returned to Drury Lane in 1782 to be praised as the greatest tragic acress ever known. With her brother, John Philip Kemble, she dominated the stage of the last decades of the eighteenth century and imposed a new formalism upon tragic acting.

So the mannered quavering of the old school gave way to the apparently spontaneous speech and movement of Garrick and

92 *A Picture of England*, p. 239.   93 P. 63.
94 *Gloucester Journal*, 4 November 1787.

D

his followers, and they, in turn, had to give place to a more artificial style. Fashions in acting styles change like everything else, and the appeal to nature means something different for every generation.

THE LONDON THEATRES. *PLATE. IV. Engraved for the U.M. for Sept.*

King Lear; Act.V. Scene the Prison, as Performd by. M.ʳBarry, &. M.ʳˢ Dancer at the Theatre Royal *in the* HayMarket.

Barry as Lear in 1767.

CHAPTER THREE

Costume

Audiences before Garrick's time had long been accustomed to seeing most of the parts in the repertoire acted in eighteenth-century dress. The apparel of hero and heroine might vaguely suggest another land or period, but the rest of the company normally appeared in contemporary clothing. The costumes were usually well made, and were sometimes finery cast off by the aristocracy. Even the small Bath theatre of 1733 could advertise that it acted in 'four suits of men's rich cloaths, and three of women's, left off by the Royal family.'[1]

The patent theatres went on using that source of supply during the managements of Garrick and John Rich. George Anne Bellamy recalled[2] that young ladies in the companies were usually dressed in the 'cast' gowns of persons of quality, and that when Rich wanted Peg Woffington to look well in the part of Roxana, he purchased a dress from the Dowager Princess of Wales: 'it was not in the least soiled, and looked very beautiful by day light, but being a straw colour, it seemed a dirty white by candle light.' This was not the happiest choice, and gradually the theatres gave up buying cast-offs that would have looked sumptuous in the daylight of Elizabethan playhouses, but were not so splendid by artificial light. Instead,

---

1 C. Price, 'Some Movements of the Bath Company,' *Theatre Notebook*, i (1946), 55–6.
2 *Apology* (2nd ed., 1785), i. 51, 206.

they took to employing their own sempstresses to make some of their most superb costumes to their own requirements.

Stage dresses were often costly: in 1769 those used by Mrs. Yates were listed at £119, by Mrs. Mattocks at £97, by Mrs. Bulkley at £68, and by Mrs. Green at £62. The total value of the women's wardrobe at Covent Garden Theatre in that year came to £2,892, and that included seven coronation robes.[3] They were looked after carefully and kept in presses. In time, the dressmakers altered them for other use. Tate Wilkinson tells us[4] that 'an old petticoat, made for a large hoop of the Duchess of Northumberland thirty years ago, would have served a Queen in the theatre for several years, then descended to a Duchess of Suffolk, afterwards made two tragedy shapes for an old rich Spaniard, and ten years after that turn and produce money to purchase thirty yards of lustring for a modern stage lady.'

Men's clothes sometimes cost even more than women's. Charlotte Lane's bill for a coat to be worn by Sparks in the part of Dr. Wolf in Cibber's *The Non Juror*, on 29 September 1755, reads:

To a Superfine full Trimm'd black cloth Coat and Breeches		14.	–
Sewing silk and Twist		4.	6
Buckram and Stays		2.	6
Frilly sleeve lining, pockets, & Interlining in ye Cuffs		2.	6
Hair Cloth, Wadding, & Poll Davy		5.	0
Dimety lining, Leather pockets, & silk garters		6.	6
4 Doz^{n} 2 Coat Death Head Buttons @	14^{d}	4.	11
13 Breast D°. @	7^{d}		8
5 Yds Black Shalloon @	2/2	10.	10
		£2. 11.	5

This outfit cost a pound more than the costume she made, in the same season, for Miss Hallam, in the breeches part of *The*

---

3 S. Rosenfeld, 'The Wardrobes of Lincoln's Inn Fields and Covent Garden,' *Theatre Notebook*, v (1950), 18.

4 *Memoirs* (York, 1790), iv. 87.

Orphan: a callimancho coat, breeches, and altered silver damask waistcoat.[5]

Women's costume, of course, sometimes drew spectators for itself alone. The German visitor, Lichtenberg, said of Mrs. Abington that 'her dress is always in the most exquisite taste. She seldom appears on the stage when the mode in genteel society does not follow her lead.'[6] Three engravings by Isaac Taylor show her in eighteenth-century clothes very suited to the parts she represented. As Phillis in Steele's *The Conscious Lovers*, she wore a costume that was plain enough to suggest an honourable simplicity, but also sufficiently handsome to be really attractive. As Lady Sadlife in Cibber's *The Double Gallant*, she was fittingly gloomy in a high-piled headdress and panniered skirt; but as Lady Betty Modish in the same playwright's *The Careless Husband*, her fashion-plate existence was indicated in full hoop and ostrich feather. It is little wonder that the *London Chronicle* remarked that Mrs. Abington, as the pattern of elegance, 'drew to the boxes an unusual number of milliners from Tavistock street.'[7]

Fashion attracted some, and merely amused others. When Foote played Lady Pentweazle, he delighted the Queen with his headdress, a yard wide and full of feathers.[8] Garrick, too, took off this extravagance, and a newspaper reported: 'the female head dress has now reached the highest degree of ridicule. It was time for the stage to lay hold of such extreme folly, and to expose it to the derision of the public. Mr. Garrick, in the part of Sir John Brute exhibited a most extraordinary lady's cap, ornamented with such a plume of feathers, ribbons of various colours, oranges and lemons, flowers, etc., so formidable a toupee, that the audience gave repeated bursts of laughter.'[9]

The managers made allowances to their leading players for

5 Folger Library MS. W. b. 473, f. 397.
6 Lichtenberg, *op. cit.*, p. 34.
7 Aug. 30–Sept. 1 1781.   8 *Chester Chronicle*, 18 July 1776.
9 *Chester Chronicle*, 12 Feb. 1776.

eighteenth-century costumes, but kept a careful eye on the way the money was spent. I judge that Garrick was deliberately restricting Mrs. Abington's spending power when, in October 1771, he repaid the sixty pounds she had laid out in clothes at the rate of seven pounds down and two pounds a week thereafter.[10] Certainly in the quarrel between Colman and Harris at Covent Garden in 1768, one of Harris's chief complaints lay in the 'incredible expence of dresses for Mrs. Yates.'[11]

Quarrels over costumes were by no means unknown. George Anne Bellamy mentions Peg Woffington's fury, when she saw Bellamy in the very modern gown just imported from Paris that she proposed to wear as the Persian Princess in Lee's *The Rival Queens, or the Death of Alexander the Great*. 'In these *robes de cours*,' she writes, 'taste and elegance were never so happily blended. Particularly in one of them, the ground of which was a deep yellow. . . . ' Mrs. Woffington was so irritable that Mrs. Bellamy promised she would never wear this gown again. So on the following evening, she appeared in an even more splendid dress and Mrs. Woffington's rage 'bordered on madness.' Rich refused to interfere, and Foote brought out a piece satirising them and called it 'The Green Room Squabble, or a Battle Royal between the Queen of Babylon and the Daughter of Darius.'[12]

Two German visitors to the London theatre, impressed by the gorgeous appearance of the costumes, were amazed to find that they were sometimes trimmed with genuine gold and silver.[13] The prodigality of these displays offended some members of the audience. 'The Plain Dealer' in *A Letter to Mr. Garrick* (? 1747)[14] complained vehemently of 'that extravagance of dress which of late glitters on the stage.—There was a time when

10 Folger Library MS. W. b. 274.
11 *A True State of the Differences subsisting between the Proprietors of Covent Garden Theatre* (1768), pp. 4–5.
12 *Apology*, ii. 207.
13 J. A. Kelly, *German Visitors to English Theaters* (Princeton, 1936), pp. 31, 65.
14 P.19.

the best actors contented themselves with a new suit at each new play, and then too thought they were very fine in tinsel lace and spangles; but some of the present heroes must not only have a new habit for every new part, but several habits for the same part, if the play continues to be acted for any number of nights: I have taken notice of one in particular, who is rarely seen twice in one garb—These habits must also be as rich as fancy can invent, or money purchase.—In fine, nothing worse will suffice to appear in even in the character of a town rake, but such as would become a Prince of the Blood on a Birth-day, or a foreign ambassador in his public entry.' Wilkinson, writing forty years later, accepted this state of things as normal, saying 'the expence for the necessary profusion of stage dresses is enormous.'[15] Not everyone was equally ready to take the new splendour for granted, and the sharp-tongued Kitty Clive showed her displeasure when Garrick appeared in a 'silver spangled tissue shape' in *Barbarossa*, by crying out, 'O my God! room! room! make room for the royal lamplighter.'[16] Yet it is only fair to say that the greater showiness which was seen early at Covent Garden under John Rich and spread to Drury Lane under Garrick, was warmly applauded by the public, and that the appeal to the eye became stronger and stronger as the century progressed. Wilkinson himself felt its force soon in his career and in rather ludicrous circumstances. Shuter thought to encourage the novice by allowing him to take the part of the Fine Gentleman in *Lethe* at a benefit night, and for two guineas was able to hire, from a costumier in Monmouth Street, 'a heavy, rich, glaring, spangled, embroidered velvet suit of clothes . . . fit for the King in *Hamlet*.' Wilkinson was so successful in the part that he was asked to play it again at another benefit night, this time for two poverty-stricken members of the company who could not afford the Monmouth Street finery. When the theatre stock was examined, Wilkinson found that all the best costumes had been handed out and he had to be content with 'a very short old suit of clothes, with a

15 *Memoirs*, iv. 86.   16 *Ibid.*, iii. 48.

black velvet ground, and broad gold flowers, as dingy as the twenty four letters on a piece of gilded gingerbread.' He took it more eagerly when he heard that Garrick had played in it years earlier, and also accepted 'an old red surtout, trimmed with a dirty white fur, and a deep skinned cape,' once worn by Giffard as Lear. To these Wilkinson added an old muff, and he hoped for loud applause. Instead, he was treated with contempt, and he left the stage 'to peals of mirth and universal hisses.'[17] Fine feathers make fine birds.

The use of the plume was abandoned during this period. Hamlet, of course, refers to the 'forest of feathers' that would get him a place in a fellowship of players, and Tom Davies explains[18] that the Prince of Denmark alluded to the large plumes that were worn 'in characters of heroism and dignity', till Garrick's 'superior taste got rid of the incumbrance.' The high-plumed turban that Garrick wore as Othello subjected him to some ridicule. According to theatrical legend, Quin thought he so strongly resembled the black servant in 'The Harlot's Progress' that he cried out, 'Here's Pompey—but where is the tea Kettle.'

The feathers were associated with two conventional costumes. One was the Roman 'shape' for actors who personified heroes of classical antiquity. Alexander the Great, as played by Barry, wore a plumed helmet, corselet and skirt, with a cloak fastened in front. Garrick's use of the same costume was the subject of one of Aaron Hill's more unfortunate letters to him:

I have been told that you dislike the Roman shapes: but hardly credit the report; because I know, that those especially, which have *robes* added, and don't lace behind, but open at the breast, like our stage *Greek* and *Persian* dresses will add grace beyond expression; and much *weight* and *fulness* to your figure—which in modern cloaths must look shortest; and yet never did, nor *can* you want sufficient *stature*, on the Theatre, where you are measur'd not by inches, but by *beauties*, and are used to fill men's eyes too copiously

---

17 *Memoirs*, i. 111–15.
18 *Dramatic Miscellanies* (1784), iii. 90–5.

to leave 'em room to see, or dream of such unreal and suppos'd deficiency.[19]

It is difficult to believe that Garrick looked taller in the Roman shape than in modern dress: the skirt and plume did not help him. In fact, one critic remarked, 'when I see him nodding under plumes, I never have less idea of a hero! and when he blusters at the head of his scene-men soldierized, he reminds me of the simile of the cock-sparrow at the head of a flock of turkies.'[20] That simile was drawn from the first scene in Fielding's *The Tragedy of Tragedies*, and the reading public of the day was so theatre-mad that it would have picked up the allusion without difficulty. It might also have recalled the frontispiece to the printed version, in which Tom Thumb was shown in his mighty littleness, almost overwhelmed by a huge plume.

Another conventional costume was the 'Turkish', adopted for all eastern and outlandish characters. Bajazet, for example, was played by Mossop in a turban with crescent and plume, caftan, baggy breaches and fur-trimmed cloak.

The 'Spanish', too, was a well-known dress, made up of puffed or slashed doublet/jacket, with knee-breeches and cloak. This was thought peculiarly suitable for villains. Another style was called 'Old English', and vaguely suggested the period 1520 to 1650. Garrick's memoranda for a performance of *The Jubilee*[21] includes a note reading '2 Men drest in Old English.' It consisted of puffed or slashed doublet and surcote, with trunk hose.[22]

Women's costume had its approximations to these styles but did not depart as much from normal eighteenth-century dress. Mrs. Yates, as Medea, wore plumes and a modified contemporary costume, and as Zaphira, turban and plumes. Mrs. Clive, as Zara, wore a huge hoop, very gaily patterned. Peg

19 *Works* (1753), ii. 247.
20 *The Theatrical Examiner* (1757), p. 27.
21 See the Huntington Library copy: K-D., vol. 332, f. 24.
22 See, also, R. J. Pentzell, "Garrick's Costuming,' *Theatre Survey*, (Pittsburgh, 1969), 18–42.

Woffington's apparel, in Mrs. Ford of *The Merry Wives of Windsor*, suggested ruff and stomacher, and completed the 'Old English' illusion with a lace cap framing the face. Empresses and queens, however, were confined to black velvet (so Mrs. Bellamy says), 'except on extraordinary occasions, when they put on an embroidered or tissue petticoat.' She also refers to the white satin dress, which *The Critic* informs us was normally worn by a heroine. She herself wore it when playing at the Glasgow Theatre, though quite clearly she would have preferred the even more usual 'black vestment'.[23]

Surviving records also show that dress could indicate calling, character, and type. John Rich's inventory of Covent Garden stock in 1744 included the following:

> Waterman's Dutch jacket and red waistcoat
> A white mantua Shepherd's dress drapery sleeves
> 2 chimney sweepers' waistcoats
> Tinker's Budget [pouch] and Apron
> 4 old Heralds coats
> Conjuror's gown
> 6 Beefeaters' coats.

The list also named costumes associated with certain theatrical characters: 'Falstaff's new dress, Falstaff's old dress, Justice Shallow's dress, Sir Hugh's old black bugle coat, King Charles' dress, Duke of Gloucester's breeches, Nump's dress, Fondlewife's hat, Clodpole's hat, the eagle's dress in Jupiter and Europa, 14 old bases [skirts] for Citizens in Julius Caesar, Aboan's linen dress in Oroonoko.'[24]

Tradition has sometimes associated the costume of the gravedigger in *Hamlet* with the many waistcoats that he stripped off before beginning his professional task, but it is clear that in the period we are discussing this was not the practice in the London patent theatres. When Thomas King played the part

23 *Apology*, i. 51; iv. 65; i. 130.
24 Add. MS. 12201, transcribed by P. H. Highfill, Jr., 'Rich's 1744 Inventory . . . ,' *Restoration & 18th Century Theatre Research*, v (Chicago, 1966), i. 11–16; ii. 18–23.

at Drury Lane in October 1796, Tate Wilkinson wrote asking him about it and received the following reply:

> As to your question—'how I dress the Grave-digger'—I affect no novelty—I follow Yates and other respectable performers whom I have formerly seen.—The Coat and upper waistcoat are of a greyish frieze; over which waistcoat I wear a broad belt—which coat, waistcoat and belt, I take off, by the assistance of my partner, and go to work in an under thick flannel waistcoat with sleeves—when in the grave, before I begin to dig, I also take off my hat, which is rather large, and cock'd in nearly a regular triangle, and put on a cap—which Cap I take from the side-pocket of my breeches, which are rather easy, *not large*. What may have been done in former times, or may be done by mummers of the present day, I am unable to say—but I have been a member of the Theatre Royal in London and Dublin seven or eight and forty years, and I have never been present when Shakespeare has been degraded, and the common sense of an audience insulted in the way you mention. I cou'd almost wish an actor to be confined to the eating bread and cheese for life, who cou'd descend to using them at the grave of Ophelia: and to be divested of his last waistcoat who cou'd so far violate propriety as to carry as many Peelings as an onion, and suppose there could be merit in taking them off. . . . [25]

What is interesting, here, is that King felt nothing but contempt for the wretched stroller who was reduced to raising a laugh by taking off the waistcoats and eating bread and cheese by the open grave. As a London professional of the highest standing, he prided himself in following the manner of performance of the respectable actors he had watched in the past.

Other costumes were associated with particular types. The miser wore square-toed shoes, and an old coat stuffed at the neck to make him look round-shouldered.[26] The description is given flesh by Maria's words in Murphy's *The Citizen* (I.i): 'He looks like the picture of Avarice, sitting with pleasure upon a bag of money and trembling for fear any body should come

[25] Folger Library MS. Box 1; 12 Oct. 1796.
[26] B. E. Barrow, 'Macklin's Costume . . . for Lovegold,' *Theatre Notebook*, xiii (1958), 67.

and take it away.—He has got square-toed shoes, and little tiny buckles, a brown coat, with small brass buttons, that looks as if it was new in my great-grand-mother's time.' He belonged to the class described in *The Theatrical Examiner* (1757): 'All the feeble old men in comedy are, I think, given us with bent back under surtout coats, a stick and squared shoes, a flat hat, and an old tye wig oddly thrown together over a carcass thus disposed, who are to laugh out in trebbles, and be all one tone and gesture.'[27]

Fops were recognised by some up-to-date extreme of fashion. Lichtenberg tells us that Garrick made Sir John Brute a fop by perching a small, beribboned, modish hat on top of his wig, and emphasising his bluster with an oaken stick.[28]

National costume, too, was sometimes employed in the theatre. Rich's list included 'Tyrolese jacketts of silk red ribbon and copper lace and red sattin Forebody's', as well as a 'blue Padua Highlander's jacket.'[29] Teague's blanket and shillelagh were all that was left, in the middle of the eighteenth century, of the old costume that had distinguished the stage Irishman.[30] The fact that Duncan (in *Macbeth*) was a Scots king was indicated in the wearing of the Thistle, and the author of *An Essay on Acting*[31] remarks sarcastically, 'I felt some pleasure at seeing Mr. Mills's *Green Ribbon and Star* in the character of Duncan: the unexpected Introduction of the *Scotch order*, was an agreeable Novelty, and discovered great Fancy in the Actor.' *Macbeth* was given at Edinburgh on 26 December 1757 with 'the characters entirely new dress'd after the manner of the Ancient Scots.'[32] What had usually been accepted in the London theatres for Scots dress may have been in Rich's list: '6 Scotch jacketts and caps 2 stuff plad sashes & 6 bonnets.' Yet when Allan Ramsay's song, 'The Highland Laddie', was published after performance at Drury Lane, an

[27] P. 82. [28] Lichtenberg, *op. cit.*, pp. 17–18.
[29] P. H. Highfill, Jr., *op. cit.*, i. 11–12.
[30] J. O. Bartley, *Teague, Shenkin and Sawney* (Cork, 1954), pp. 103, 126.
[31] (1744), p. 23.
[32] J. C. Dibdin, *Annals of the Edinburgh Stage* (Edinburgh, 1888), pp. 95–6.

The Highland Laddie. *Sung at the Theatre in Drury Lane.*

The Lawland Lads think they are fine, But O they're vain and idly gaudy, How much unlike that graceful Mein, and manly Looks of my Highland Laddie: O my bonny Highland Laddie, my handsome smiling Highland Laddie, may Heav'n still guard and Love reward, The Lowland Lass and her Highland Laddie.

2
If I were free at will to chuse,
  To be the wealthiest Lawland Lady,
I'd take young Dormald *without Trews,*
With Bonnet blue and belted Plaidy.
O my bonny. &c.

3
The bravest Beau in Borrows Town,
  In a' his Airs with Arts made ready,
Compair'd to him he's but a Clown,
He's finer far in's tartan Plaidy.
O my bonny. &c.

4
O'er Benty Hill with him I'll run,
  And leave my Lawland kin & dady,
Frae Winters Cauld & Sommers Sun,
He'll screen me with his Highland Plaidy.
O my bonny. &c.

5
A painted Room and Silken Bed,
  May please a Lawland Laird & Lady,
But I can kiss and be as glad,
Behind a Bush in's Highland Plaidy.
O my bonny. &c.

6
Few Compliments between us pass,
  I ca him my dear Highland Laddie,
And he ca's me his Lawland Lass,
Sine rows me in beneath his Plaidy.
O my bonny. &c.

7
Nae greater Joy I'll eir pretend
  Than that his Love prove true & steady,
Like mine to him which nier shall end,
While Heav'n preserve my Highland Laddie.
O my bonny. &c.

A song by Allan Ramsey to music by Michael Arne.

COSTUME

engraving showed the laddie in a kilt. Perhaps this was artist's
licence: whether or not the kilt was worn in stage entertainments has certainly been the subject of some discussion.
Macklin's production of *Macbeth* at Covent Garden Theatre on
23 October 1773 is thought to show the first movement towards
historical realism in the patent theatres, because its dresses were
described as 'new, elegant, and of a sort hitherto unknown to a
London audience, but exceedingly proper.'[33] Miss M. St. Clare
Byrne has proved that the kilt was not worn in the second act
by quoting a correspondent of the *St. James's Chronicle*, 23–26
October, who mentioned that Macklin pulled up 'the waist
band of his Breeches as he comes forward to invite his Nobles
to the Banquet.' She goes on to suggest that the Scots costume
worn by Macbeth and Banquo in the first act was a tunic, plaid,
tartan stockings and Balmoral bonnet; and that in Act II the
same characters wore knee-breeches and jacket, with a plaid
and an Order of the Thistle to give them local colour.[34] So
this does not appear to have been a revolutionary production
in the history of the theatre, but rather an attempt at novelty
which was only one move beyond customary practice. It
perfectly represented theatrical taste of the period in that it
moved rather tentatively away from older, accepted conventions.

The date at which a wish for propriety in costuming began
to influence the managers is also rather controversial. One of
the early complaints appears in John Hill's *The Actor* (1755):
'the dress of the player is another article in which we expect a
conformity to nature; but this we expect in vain, especially in
the women; the characters of an inferior kind, are always
overdressed.'[35] This, too, was emphasised in Robert Lloyd's
The Actor (1760).

To suit the Dress demands the Actor's Art,
Yet there are those who overdress the Part,

33 *Morning Chronicle*, 25 Oct. 1773.
34 'The Stage Costuming of Macbeth in the Eighteenth Century,'
Studies in English Theatre History (1952), pp. 52–64.   35 P. 255.

54

To some prescriptive Right gives settled Things,
Black Wigs to Murd'rers, feather'd hats to Kings,
But *Michael Cassio* might be drunk enough,
Tho' all his Features were not grim'd with Snuff.
Why shou'd *Poll Peachum* shine in sattin Cloaths?
Why ev'ry Devil dance in scarlet Hose?

Some rationality was demanded. The author of *A Letter from the Rope-Dancing Monkey* (1767) remarked that Queen Margaret in *The Earl of Warwick* was 'improperly drest, for the afflicted consort of a monarch in captivity. The absurdity of giving Spanish habits for the English dresses at that time, is judiciously exposed in a letter, lately published in the [Public] Ledger'.[36] In the same year, Hugh Kelly's *The Babler*[37] asked: 'What business has a party of English foot guards to attend upon a Persian emperor? Or is it a reason that a prince should not be habited like a prince, because the actor who appears in the character has but 30/- a week. . . . [Who can endure to see] the persons of one single family drest in the manner of half a dozen countries? The probability of the fiction becomes destroyed by means of these slovenly inattentions, and Drury Lane or Covent Garden, stare us, continually in the face, when we want to be in Spain or in France, in Italy or Illyria?' When Sheridan's *The Duenna* was presented in December 1775, there was a similar complaint about the costume of the friars: 'Any one the least conversant in Ecclesiastical Reading, or that has ever landed on the Continent, must be sensible that the Jacobins, or Friars, are never dressed in blue; the former wearing a black Habit mixed with white on the fore Part; and the latter either a brown one, as in France, or a black one, as in Italy or other hot countries.[38] Clearly the writer's pleasure must have been marred by seeing the wrong-coloured costume, but in this grievance he must have represented only a very small minority.

It is fair to say, I think, that with the desire for appropriate

---

36 P. 9. 37 P. 248.
38 'Spectator' in the *St. James's Chronicle*, 12–14 Dec. 1775.

costume went a far less insistent demand for what we now call historical realism in the dressing of stage characters. As early as 1731, Aaron Hill had put forward some suggestions for the costuming of his play *Athelwold*, set in Anglo-Saxon times: 'Leolyn, because a Briton, ought not to have his habit *Saxon* all; The rest have the authority of Verstegan's *Antiquities*, for the ground-work of their appearance; only I need not observe to you, that some *Heightenings* were necessary, because beauty must be joined to *propriety*, where the decoration of the stage, is the purpose to be provided for.' His qualifying the statement was sensible, and he went on to make another shrewd point in the same letter: 'The Furrs, which you will observe pretty frequent, in these *figures*, are a prime *distinction*, in the *old Saxon* habits; and they will have something of a *grandeur*, not without beauty; but they need not be real furrs—many cheap imitations will have the same effect, at the distance they will be seen from.'[39] This was to be an important consideration as the playhouses grew in size, for improved artificial lighting gave a glow even to the cheaper materials.

Hill's interest in historical costume was not echoed very frequently in this period. Paul Hifferman came nearest to it, when he recommended, in *Dramatic Genius* (1772),[40] that managers should study ancient works, and more recent studies by writers like Octavius Ferrari, so as to know 'how to dress plays, taken from the Greek and Roman histories, etc., as well as from the histories of remoter nations of the world. . . . From Potter's *Greek*, and Kennet's *Roman*, antiquities, he can get sufficient instruction relative to their religious ceremonies, triumphal entries, processions, etc.'

There was some opposition expressed to this line of thinking. Count Algarotti was firmly of the opinion that costuming ought to avoid any suspicion of pedantry. Lichtenberg agreed: 'If we are not vastly learned, ancient costumes on the stage are too reminiscent of a disguise worn at a masquerade.' He added the useful point that much was lost in a garb that did not

[39] *Works* (1753), i. 89–90. [40] Pp. 214–15.

gratify youthful vanity or the recollection of it, and made his case for modern costume on sentimental as well as practical grounds. 'Our French coats have long ago been advanced to the dignity of a tunic, and their creases to the importance of a play of features; while all wrestling, writhing, fencing and falling in an unfamiliar dress we can, indeed, understand but not feel sensibly.'[41] In these perceptive lines there was a realisation that for the actor freedom of movement must be of first importance, that the costume should therefore be based on tunic and trunks or breeches, and that the nearer these seemed in appearance to eighteenth-century clothes, the more easily were they accepted.

Garrick's own attitude to the subject is not unlike that of Lichtenberg. With his remarkable flair for the theatre, he realised almost by instinct, certainly by observation, what was and what was not acceptable to his audiences. Lichtenberg noticed this, and remarked that Garrick was able to 'gauge to a nicety the taste of his fellow-countrymen, certainly attempts nothing on the stage without good reason, and besides, has a whole house full of ancient costumes.'[42] Yet his first steps towards historical realism came only at the very end of his career, and even they were not clearly defined.

He was undoubtedly well read concerning the costume of past ages. His library contained Verstegan's *Restitution of Decayed Intelligence in Antiquities* (1653) with the illustrations of Anglo-Saxon costume that Hill had mentioned. He owned Rowe's illustrated edition (1709) of Shakespeare's works. He also had P. Picart's *Ceremonies et Costumes Religieuses du tous les Peuples du Monde* (1723), *A Collection of Dresses of Different Nations, Antient and Modern, also of the Principal Characters of the English Stage* (1757), J. B. Greuze's *Divers Habillements suivant le Costume d'Italie ornés de fonds* (1768), and Strutt's *Manners, Customs, Arms, and Habits of the People of England* (1776).[43]

---

41 Lichtenberg, *op. cit.*, pp. 22–3.   42 *Ibid.*, p. 21.
43 Lots 2397, 2272, 1878, 767, 1074, 2373, in *A Catalogue of the Library of David Garrick, Esq. . . . sold by Auction by Mr. Saunders . . . on Wednesday, April 23d . . .* [1823].

E

With such a wealth of information at hand, Garrick could have initiated a movement towards greater authenticity had he wished to do so. Towards the end of his life, he mentioned that he had a 'design to exhibit the Characters in old dresses in Macbeth;'[44] but this came to nothing. Just before he left the stage, however, he presented a performance of *King Lear*, in which the cast was said to be 'judiciously habited in Old English dresses.' A report in the *London Chronicle*,[45] added that 'Lear's was more majestic than usual, and in our opinion much more in character.' The significance of the sentence is probably to be found in an emphasis on the way in which dress enhances character-revelation, rather than on the correctness of the costume from an historical point of view.

This appears to be in line with Garrick's thinking on the subject: what was always important was that the type of character should be quickly recognised in its dress. An earlier example of this is to be seen in the 'hussar' costume that he wore as Tancred in Thomson's *Tancred and Sigismunda*. It comprised frogged military jacket and knee-breeches with fur cap, sash, and fur-trimmed cape. We should now be tempted to call it Ruritanian, and it gives an immediate impression of the dashing soldier.

Paintings reveal Garrick as Richard III in what approximated to the 'Old English' style: doublet and breastplate, trunk and hose. Engravings show him in short jacket and knee-breeches in the Spanish mode. While this is a reminder that generalising from illustrations is difficult because the artist may be pleasing his own fancy rather than representing faithfully the character in the theatre, it also indicates something of the mixture of styles that was possible in the old conventions. Support for this is to be found in Garrick's letter to his partner in which he proposed to outdo Covent Garden

44 *The Letters of David Garrick* (ed. Little and Kahrl, Cambridge, Mass., 1963), p. 838.
45 12–23 May 1776.

with a production of *King John* in which the characters were to be dressed 'half old English, half modern.'[46]

The truth is that Garrick was not an antiquary, and that he shared the prejudices of Algarotti and Lichtenberg against a pedantic fussiness about historical accuracy. He found nothing displeasing in playing some of the most famous Shakespearean roles in eighteenth-century costume. He acted Romeo in the clothes of his day, wore the normal black court-suit as Hamlet, and if Benjamin Wilson's painting of the storm scene is accurate, white shirt, red coat, russet waistcoat and breeches for the part of Lear. Only when he played Macbeth was severe complaint levelled against his costume. A hostile critic said that he looked too much like a '*modern fine gentleman*, so that when you came among the Witches in the 4th Act, you looked like a Beau, who had unfortunately slipped his Foot and tumbled into a Night Cellar, where a Parcel of Old Women were boiling Tripe for their Supper.'[47] Since the witches were played by men with beards, gowns, and coifs, the encounter sounds an entertaining one.

So, although Aaron Hill had thoughtfully noted that eighteenth-century dress relaxed 'the pomp of Tragedy and, the generality, being led by the *eye* can conceive nothing extra-ordinary, where they see nothing uncommon,'[48] Garrick persisted in wearing it and was justified in doing so. He knew that most people in the audience would take it for granted, and that in any case he could make them forget it in the intensity of his acting. Garrick's main business, after all, was to show psychological perception, the way in which the mind disguises itself.

In sum, the period saw no revolution in general attitudes towards stage costume. Eighteenth-century clothes were worn in most plays, though a few leading characters might be dressed

46 *The Letters of David Garrick*, p.152.
47 Quoted from the *St. James's Chronicle*, 30 Oct. 1773, by K. A. Burnim, *David Garrick, Director* (Pittsburgh, 1961), pp. 121-2.
48 *Works*, i. 190.

in stock garb that represented—at a distance—some historical period. When a demand was made occasionally that dress should be 'appropriate', it was usually caused by a desire for local colour and not by the taste for antiquarian exactness that was to develop towards the turn of the century.

Even so, some apology had to be made for apparent oddity, and we find Mrs. Yates saying in the epilogue to *The Orphan of China*, 'Ladies, excuse my dress—'tis true Chinese.'

Garrick as Richard III.

CHAPTER FOUR

The Attraction of Spectacle

Eighteenth-century Europe witnessed a new sophistication in stage settings that was largely due to Italian artists. The Bibiena family, for example, had a profound influence on the development of theatrical scenery as an art form. Fortunes were spent on festivals and opera productions in Italy, France, and Austria, and a new interest was taken in lighting as a means of focussing the audience's attention.

Count Algarotti, in his *Essay on Opera* (1768),[1] warmly praised the innovations:

Serlio,[2] from whose treatise upon scenery there may be nevertheless some good hints taken, did not sufficiently consider how, without the assistance of relievos in wood, we might conquer all the difficulties of perspective; and how, in very confined situations, we could represent the appearance of extensive space; but to such a pitch the science of deceiving the eye has been improved in our time. The introduction, especially, of accidental points or rather the invention of viewing scenes by the angle, produces the finest effects imaginable; but that requires the nicest judgement to bring properly into practice. Ferdinando Bibiena was the inventor of those scenes, which, by the novelty of the manner, drew the eyes of all the curious upon him. They soon began to look upon, as unpleasing objects for the stage,

---

[1] Pp. 74–5.
[2] Sebastiano Serlio (1473–1554) studied the Greek and Roman theatres as inspiration for his architectural designs on canvas flats. His complete writings were published in Venice in 1584, edited by G. D. Scamozzi.

those streets and narrow passages, those galleries that were always made to lead to its center, there at once to limit the spectators' imagination and sight . . .

The old style, with its emphasis on painted buildings that seems to grow smaller as they converged at some distant centre, offended common sense when an actor stood at the focal point and appeared much bigger than the buildings on either side of him. Algarotti himself put the case neatly: 'giants dwindle by degrees as they come forward, and are dwarfed down to their native size, as they approach nearer to us.'[3]

England was always slow to pick up foreign ways, and Thornhill's designs for the opera, *Arsinoe, Queen of Cyprus* (1705), have been shown[4] to represent an old-fashioned set with shutter and side wings in rigid symmetry. The new look was asymmetrical, and wings that were really parallel to the front of the stage, looked diagonal and gave a remarkable impression of height. Possibly it was introduced to English opera-goers by Robert Clerici, son of one of Ferdinando Bibiena's pupils, and designer at the King's Theatre between 1716 and 1720, or by Giovanni Servandoni, who contributed scenes for the same opera house between 1721 and 1723.[5]

Servandoni was employed by John Rich at Covent Garden for some time after 1747 and some of the sets he created were used there after his death in 1766. The palace of Pluto in *The Rape of Proserpine* on 4th November 1769 and the palace of Sylphs in J. A. Fisher's *Sylphs* on 3 January 1774, were greatly admired. The best account that I have been able to find of an opera production in which the new perspective and Servandoni's scenery are mentioned, appears in the *London Chronicle*, 11–14 November 1758, and is worth quoting at length because it makes a significant distinction between the appeal of spectacle in opera and in comedy or tragedy, and gives many more

3 P. 85.
4 J. Laver, *Drama: Its Costume and Decor* (1951), pp. 159–60.
5 For their work, see S. Rosenfeld and E. Croft-Murray, 'A Checklist of Scene Painters . . .,' *Theatre Notebook* xix (1964–5), 19, xx (1965–6), 36–7.

details than are usually available concerning the performance itself. It describes the first presentation of Galuppi's *Attalo* at the King's Theatre:

I shall begin with observing, that an Opera has in one particular a manifest advantage over almost every theatrical entertainment, by admitting of that kind of shew and decoration, which if not absolutely rejected by the other daughters of the Drama, is at least generally speaking, forced upon them: that is to say, though we sometimes see triumphs and processions in a few of our tragedies and comedies, yet the best judges have always looked on them as childish and ridiculous; Whereas the only design of an Opera being to delight, that gay finery which looks so unbecoming and out of character upon her two elder sisters, is a necessary part of her dress. . . .

. . . I shall hardly attempt to do any thing more in the present essay than to assure them that the finest scenes, the finest panto-mime hitherto invented, even by that father of pantomimes himself, the manager of Covent-garden playhouse [John Rich], are con-siderably inferior to those in the opera of *Attalo*; but particularly, in the first act, where Semiramis enters in a triumphal car, supported by Medean and Bactrian slaves, and surrounded by a number of Assyrian soldiers who carry the spoils and trophies of an enemy which she is supposed lately to have conquered, we are presented with the scene of a square; not a dead piece of painted canvas, but one in which the prospective [*sic*] is executed in so masterly a manner, that one would almost swear it was something more than a *deceptio visus*; to which, by the way, a pedestrian statue, which is elevated in the centre of the buildings, does not a little contribute.

Scenes of this kind are seldom if ever to be seen in a common theatre, where the other charges are so large and numerous, as well as the price so confined, that the profits of such a pompous apparatus would by no means answer the expence; the place in our English plays also is too often varied to allow of it; besides the business of these stages is, properly speaking, to provide the understanding with substantial food, not to treat it with conserves and sweetmeats, and from this reason it proceeds that dances, which at the playhouse are only made use of as a garnish, are at the opera (which may not unaptly be compared to a dessert or a col[l]ation) one of the principal parts of the entertainment.

63

. . . In the first dance, the scene of which, by the way, may more properly be called an emulation than a copy of nature, being that of a forest half cut down, where the trees are represented in the liveliest manner, and the prospect of clouds and blue mountains extended to an amazing distance; Forti and Bononi, in the characters of a woodman and his wife, carry the grotesque to a most entertaining degree of extravagance. Bononi is allowed to excel in this way every one who has gone before her; for Galini, as his genius is very different, so it is greatly preferable to this. His dancing indeed may be considered as a kind of dumb musick since there is hardly a note which he does not express by some significant gesture. Carlini, his partner, is pretty much in the same mode, and when they appear after the second act in a very extensive plain, interspersed with villages, there cannot be imagined two more agreeable figures. But the third and last ballet, in which the four principal dancers come out together, surpasses all the rest. The prospect is that of a rock, which being open in two or three different places, discovers a wide river, and, in appearance, at least half a mile long, the transparency of the water is so well imitated, that we see the shadows of several flags and bullrushes, which grow upon it; nor is a distant village, which appears at one side, a small addition to the beauty of the view: down this rock came the figure dancers, who are met at the door of a cottage by Signor Galini and his friends; it is a kind of rural feast, and the music is so antic and lively, that that alone would be sufficient I should think, to put an audience into a good humour.

I had forgot to mention a scene in this Opera which is remarkably beautiful; I am told it was painted by the celebrated Salvandoni,[6] and is the representation of a magnificent hall, adorned with arms and trophies.

This is a remarkably interesting document because it expresses so clearly the normal critical attitude of the mid-eighteenth century towards spectacle. Scenery and costume should be as magnificent as possible because opera, ballet, and pantomime, appeared to be rather superficial entertainments that needed to please the eye. Comedy and tragedy could dispense with such adventitious aids for several reasons, the most important being the depth of meaning in their texts.

[6] Servandoni.

The writer also brought out another good point: the patent theatres, in the very number of their performances, could seldom afford to mount them with such splendour as the King's Theatre. Besides, the opera house appealed to a discerning or fashionable few who could pay heavily for their favourite pleasures. Drury Lane and Covent Garden necessarily sought support from the multitude at much lower charges.

Consequently when we read of a Drury Lane opera, we expect a less impressive display of scenery. An example may be found in Arne's 'new English opera', *Artaxerxes*, that was given its first performance on 2 February 1762, with new costumes but not with new sets. The list of scenes reads: 'An inner garden belonging to the Palace of the King of Persia', 'The Royal Apartments,' 'A Hall of Royal Council with a Throne', 'A Prison', 'Mandane's apartments', 'A Temple and Throne, with a Crown and Scepter; the Image of the Sun, with a lighted Altar.' All these could be supplied from stock, if we accept a contemporary description[7] of its usual categories: 'The stage should be furnished with a complete number of painted scenes sufficient to answer the purposes of all the plays in the stock, in which there is no great variety, being easily reduced to the following classes. 1st, Temples. 2dly, Tombs. 3rdly, City walls and gates. 4thly, Outside of Palaces. 5thly, Insides of Palaces. 6thly, Streets. 7thly Chambers. 8thly, Prisons. 9thly, Gardens. And 10thly, Rival prospects of groves, forests, desarts, etc. All these should be done by a master, if such can be procured . . . to avoid offending a judicious eye. If, for some particular purpose, any other scene is necessary, it can be got up occasionally.' The writer expresses a point of view that seems to have been common in the first half of the period: costs could be cut by using old scenes, even when they were not entirely appropriate; and only occasionally were new scenes to be commissioned as a special adornment. Looking back to this period, Tate Wilkinson said[8] that 'it was very uncommon

7 *The Case of the Stage in Ireland* (Dublin, 1758), p. 35.
8 *Memoirs* (York, 1790), iv. 91.

The set for O'Hara's *Midas, an English Burletta* (1764), II. 4.

formerly for new plays to have more than what we term stock scenery: There is one scene at Covent Garden from 1747 to this day in the Fop's Fortune, etc., which has wings and flat, of Spanish figures at full length, and two folding doors in the middle: I never see these wings slide on but I feel as if seeing my old acquaintance unexpectedly.' He went on to contrast this economy with theatre practice in the last decade of the century, when new scenery was provided for most new pieces.

It also seems certain that, in the first half of the period, comparatively few sets were used in presenting comedy and tragedy. If we look through a sample of printed texts, we shall find that, for the most part, they limit their action to one or two localities. Glover's *Boadicia* (1753) takes place at 'the British Camp before the tent of Dunmorix', and his *Medea* (1761) is set 'in the citadel of Corinth between a grove sacred to Juno, and the royal palace, with a distant prospect of the sea.' John Brown's *Barbarossa* (1755) records, 'Scene, the Royal Palace of Algiers', and his *Athelstan* (1758), 'Scene, the Danish Camp near London.' The first and third acts of Whitehead's *Creusa* (1754) were given in 'the Vestibule of the Temple of Apollo,' and the second, fourth, and fifth acts in 'a Laurel Grove adjoining.' Garrick's *The Guardian* (1759) used two sets: 'A Hall in Mr. Heartly's house' and 'A Library'. Samuel Johnson's *Irene* (1749) does not name a place of action, but we can discover from his draft outline[9] of the play that he had two locations in mind: 'a garden near the walls of Constantinople' and 'Irene's appartments'.

By the seventies far greater variety of scenery was offered. Although Murphy's *The Grecian Daughter* (1772) contains no details of the setting at the opening of his first, fourth, and fifth acts, he more than makes up for this by providing a number of other scenes: 'a wild romantic Scene, amidst overhanging Rocks; a Cavern on one side', 'the inside of a cavern', 'Opens a cell in the back scene', 'a rampart near the

9 *Poems* (ed. E. L. McAdam, Jr. with G. Milne, New Haven and London, 1964), 220, 225.

harbour,' 'a temple, with a monument in the middle', 'Inside of a Temple', 'the citadel', 'another part of the city'. Newspaper report picked out two of them for special praise: 'the representation of the city of Syracuse, with a view of the sea; and the Temple scene, with a mausoleum, in particular, are extremely well executed.'[10] Fewer sets are to be found in Dow's *Sethona* (1774), but they, too, were greatly liked. They consisted of 'the Temple of Osiris, at Memphis', 'Sethona's apartment,' 'the Catacombs', 'the court before a Prison,' and were said to be 'much superior to those of any modern Tragedy. . . . The scene of the Temple of Osiris, and the View of the Egyptian Catacombs were particularly admired.'[11]

Few of the subjects were new, and their attractiveness lay rather in the fact that they were 'done by a master.' Not every designer was a Servandoni, but a number of the scenographers at the patent houses were certainly of more than average competence. George Lambert is better remembered as the founder of the Beef Steak Club than as a devoted servant of Covent Garden theatre up to 1761. Nicholas Dall worked with him there from 1757, and was later joined by John Inigo Richards. G. B. Cipriani collaborated with them in 1771 and 1772. At Drury Lane, the names of John French, Pierre Royer, Robert Carver, are less resounding; but, after 1771, they reflected some of the glory associated with Philippe Jacques de Loutherbourg.[12] James Canter painted at the Haymarket as well as at the King's Theatre, and, since this fact has not been previously established, its source may be worth quoting. The *London Chronicle*, 19–21 September 1772, reported that in the second act of Foote's *The Nabob*, 'a new scene of the Nabob's hall is presented for the reception of the Mayor and Electors of the Borough of Bribem; this scene was painted by Mr. Canter, a disciple of the celebrated [Antonio] Jolli.'

In the nature of things, few examples of their work may now

10   *The London Stage*, 4 (ed. G. W. Stone), p. 1610.   11   *Ibid.*, 1787.
12   See S. Rosenfeld and E. Croft-Murray, *op. cit.* xix, 15, 18, 49, 55, 104–5, 142, 145.

be seen. There are plenty of engravings of theatrical subjects, Shakespearean and otherwise during this period, but they often are truer to the engraver's imagination than to an actual stage setting. It would therefore be very interesting to know the whereabouts of two pictures by Nicholas Dall that were exhibited at the Society of Artists in 1770.[13] Item 32 was 'A scene of the shipwreck in the new Comedy of the Brothers', and item 189 was 'A View of Stratford on Avon, as it appeared at the last Jubilee in honour of Shakespeare.' Both appear to have a good theatrical pedigree.

Information about the stock scenery at Covent Garden as early as 1741 may be found in John Rich's inventory,[14] though unfortunately its list of paintings is nothing like so comprehensive as its detailing of costumes and properties. Several of the sets are associated with the name of John Harvey[15] who, for three years before his death in 1735, was employed there. 'Harvey's hall' and palace are mentioned, and so are twelve curtain wings, an arch and a figure from the palace. Clearly the set was still very useful for any play that required a court background.

Other scenes were not listed as by any particular painter. Shakespearean sets included the Rialto, Othello's new hall, and Macbeth's 'car'. Among the properties were 'a tomb in Timon', Macbeth's table, Banquo's trap with barrel, and a pedestal for *The Winter's Tale*.

Many 'pieces' are noted. They represented a country house, church, inn yard, short village, cottage and long village, eight moonlight wings, a study of books, the body of a ship, and a sea port. The store also included six garden pieces, hedge, stile, and fence; six tent pieces; a cornfield in six pieces; and six waves; as well as four orange trees in pots, a haycock in two pieces, two shore pieces, and a dunghill.

13 A. Graves, *The Society of Artists* . . . (1907), p. 69.
14 Add. MS. 12201, transcribed by P. H. Highfill, Jr., in *Restoration and 18th Century Theatre Research* (Chicago), v (1966), i. 7–17; ii. 17–26; vi. (1967), i. 28–35.
15 S. Rosenfeld and E. Croft-Murray, *op. cit.*, xix, 60.

Properties associated with specified plays were a chair in *Oroonoko*, a chariot in *Comus*, a cottage and two trees in *Margery*, a bridge in *The Rehearsal*, a fallen tree in *The Dragon of Wantly*, with two oxen and four furrows for *Justin*. 'A piece with reeds' had been made for *Pan and Syrinx*.

Rich's lists also contained notes of 'six pair of cloudings, fixed to battens with barrels, weights, and ropes.' These were the hanging pieces that represented ceiling or sky, and they are sometimes named as belonging to a particular entertainment, as in 'the sky border to arch' for *The Coronation*. 'Three hill borders' are also catalogued.

Other means of achieving theatrical illusion were 'a great travelling machine used in *Orpheus*', a middle trap, a grave trap with two weights and iron hooks, and a great counterpoise to all the traps that was able to take a strain of 487 pounds. All of them were of great importance in creating spectacular effects since they enabled the stage crew to make transformations and disappearances, 'sinkings and risings', so quickly that the spectator gave himself up to accepting with wonder the marvels he had witnessed.

Another device that helps us to understand why foreign visitors were impressed by the rapidity and skill in scene changing, was the groove, generally used in English theatres. Four or six scenes on each side of the stage could be speedily thrust in, or pulled back along, these channels that ran in the floor.

The backscene was sometimes rolled down by hand (as may have been true of Rich's 'a sea back cloth') or might be a piece of practicable scenery. For an example of the latter, we have to go to Murphy's *The Orphan of China* (1759). The stage directions in the second act read: 'Two large Folding-gates in the Back-scene are burst open by the Tartars, and then enter Timurkan with his Train.' In the fifth act, we read: 'The great folding doors open in the back scene. The corpse is brought forward, Zamti lying on the couch and clasping the dead body.' Neither of these directions appears in Murphy's source,

Voltaire's *L'Orphelin de la Chine* (1755), and it is obvious that these entrances were introduced to suit English conventions.

Rich's inventory also contains some references to scenery and properties used in pantomime. This is not surprising, since Rich (as 'Lun') was the great harlequin of the age, a specialist in what he called 'Italian mimic scenes.' Among the sets were representations of Hell and Medusa's cave, as well as the inside and outside of Merlin's cave. A transformation scene is indicated in the 'front of a garden that changes to [a] house.' The properties included the dragon in Thurmond's *Harlequin Doctor Faustus*, and a gibbet tree from the same writer's *Apollo and Daphne*. A magician's chair and Pluto's trap were available, and so were 'Ceres's chariot' and 'a vinegret cupid's chariot'. The list also includes a 'catt chariot' from Theobald's *Harlequin a Sorcerer.*

This particular pantomime dated from January 1725, remained a favourite for many years, and was revived at Covent Garden in 1752. Fortunately a summary of its attractions at this later year is extant, and indicates how pantomime rivalled and even surpassed the opera house in achieving spectacular effects. Themes, like this one, that involved magic, gave a certain credibility to the more arbitrary juxtapositions of pantomime, but even so the genre presents an extraordinary medley. Here is the record[16] of the attractions of *Harlequin a Sorcerer* in 1752:

After the overture, as the curtain draws up, the first scene presents us with a group of witches exercising their orgies in a wilderness by moonlight. After a few songs, Harlequin crosses the stage, riding in the air between two witches upon a long pole, and jumps in among them—Then you have a dance of witches, where you may be sure a proper use is made of their broomsticks.

Next you see the bricklayers and their men going to work, which now marks the time of our drama to be morning.—Harlequin then stands before a balcony, serenading Columbine, who appears to him; but, as he is climbing up, he is surpris'd by Pantaloon, who comes out opening the door, and Harlequin pops in. Hence a warm

16 *Gentleman's Magazine* xxii (1752), 52-3.

pursuit ensues of Columbine and our heroe by Pantaloon and his servants. The next scene is of an house half built, with real scaffolding before it, and the men at work upon it. Columbine retires behind a pile of bricks: our hero mounts a ladder, and presently down comes the scaffolding with the men and all upon it.

You next come to a garden wall: where, as Columbine retires under it, Harlequin is turn'd into an old woman, and the scene converted into a wall with ballads and coloured wooden prints strung upon it, with a large wicker chair, in which Harlequin seats himself, supposed to be selling them. The servant comes in, buys a ballad; and here a slight satirical hint is levelled at the song of *I love Sue, and Sue loves*—introduced in the rival HARLEQUIN RANGER of t'other house.

We have now a most delightful perspective of a farm-house, whence you hear the coots in the water as at a distance.—Several rustics with their doxies come on; and Mr. *Lowe* sings an excellent song, to which all join in chorus, *to celebrate harvest home*.—This scene remov'd, a constable comes on, with the bricklayer's men, who have a warrant to take up Harlequin: Then you have a distant view of a barley mow and barn; several swains dancing before it, with Harlequin and Columbine. The constable and followers opportunely coming in, Columbine is seized and carried home by Pantaloon.

When they are in the house, the servant after many dumb gestures introduces a large ostrich, which has a very good effect upon the audience; but perhaps would have had a greater, had we not discovered by the extremities, that it was Harlequin, whose legs and thighs appear under the body. This I suppose could not be remedied, as the extremities of this bird are very small in proportion. Besides, Columbine by this means discovers him; and, after having made the whole house ring with applause by playing several tricks, (such as kissing Columbine, biting the servant, and the like,) they morrice off both together.

We are then carried to a back-part of the farm-house, which turns into a shed, where in an instant you have the view of a copper with a fire burning under it. Harlequin changes himself into an old washerwoman, and on striking a mound raised on flints mixed with earth, it is immediately turned into a washing-tub and stand; then opening a door, he shews us an horse with real linnen upon it, which is drawn out in many folds to a considerable length upon the stage.

Pantaloon and servant come in, and after being soused with the soapsuds, are driven off by the supposed washer woman with a bowl of boiling-water from the copper, to the no small diversion of both galleries. Columbine then comes forth from her retreat, and goes off with her sweetheart.

But the constable at last catches him; he tumbles down 'midst his guards, and so slips away from 'em.—We then see a fence of boards, as before a building, (excellently well painted,) which in a moment is converted to a gilt Equestrian statue. Harlequin is discovered to bestride the horse, as I remember by his sneezing: Pantaloon's servant goes to climb up by the head, which directly bends its neck and bites him: he next tries to get up by the hindleg, which in springing back gives him a most terrible kick, and the poor dog is carried off with his face all over blood and beaten to pieces.

After this, a scene drops, and gives us a prospect of ruinous rugged cliffs, with two trees hanging over them, beautifully executed. The same witches come in again, and, after singing a little while, retire. Then Harlequin appears disconsolate and prostrate upon a couch in an elegant apartment: lightning flashes; and four devils, in flame-coloured stockings, mount through trapdoors, surround him with double-tongued forks, and the whole stage with the scenery and all upon it, rises up gradually, and is carried all together into the air.

Here the Pantomime ends; and the scrupulous critic must not nicely enquire into the reasons, why Harlequin is carried upwards into the infernal regions; nor why Pluto with his fair Proserpine descends in a magnificent throne afterwards, into a fine pavillion.— After a song or two, an imp brings him word, that poor Harly is trapped, at last; but the black-bearded monarch says, every thing shall be jolly.—Then the stage is extended to a prodigious depth, closing with a prospect of fine gardens, and a temple. We are entertained a while with the agility of Mess. *Cook*, *Grandchamps*, Mademoiselles *Camargo*, *Hilliard*, and others; then with a grand chorus; lastly, with a low bow from the performers.—And so down drops the curtain.

Some critics were scrupulous enough to enquire after reasons, and to be dissatisfied with what they found. Pope devoted some lines of *The Dunciad* (1743)[17] to describing the place of panto-

17 III. 231–6.

F

mime in the reign of Dullness, and well suggested its silliness:

All sudden, Gorgons hiss, and Dragons glare,
And ten horn'd fiends and Giants rush to war.
Hell rises, Heav'n descends, and dance on Earth:
Gods, imps, and monsters, music, rage and mirth,
A fire, a jigg, a battle, and a ball,
Till one wide conflagration swallows all.
. . .
Immortal Rich! how calm he sits at ease
'Mid snows of paper, and fierce hail of pease;
And proud his Mistress' orders to perform,
Rides in the whirlwind, and directs the storm.

The absurdity of pantomime and its appeal to the unthinking were frequently mentioned in the next thirty years. *The Theatrical Campaign* (1767)[18] remarked: 'To criticise a pantomime, according to its present plan, is to approve or censure the scene-shifters, and trap-door drawers, the agility of a leap, or the clumsiness of a fall.' It found the 'constant running across the stage with imaginary red-hot pokers, Scrub's ridiculous un-variegated blunders' very tedious. What delighted some play-goers and disgusted others is obvious from a description of Mrs. Goulding's kitchen in *Harlequin-Skeleton* at Covent Garden in 1772: 'on the entry of Pantaloon and the Clown in pursuit of Harlequin, the table rises and throws off its contents; the beer barrel dances in, together with two or three large jars or pans; the clock, table, chairs, and cupboard, join in the festive bound; and the crockery on the dresser and shelves fly off, and crack into pieces musical concert.'[19]

A balanced criticism of these entertainments may be found in 'Kitt Comment's' remarks on *The Rites of Hecate; or, Harlequin in the Moon*: 'This Pantomime (if any Pantomime can be allowed a Scruple of Merit) has no inconsiderable Claim to the Approbation of every Spectator that lays by his Understanding for a while, or good-naturedly comes without any Under-standing at all; for though there are some palpable Imitations

[18] Pp. 13–14.   [19] *London Chronicle*, 30 Jan.–1 Feb. 1772.

in it, yet it abounds with a Variety of agreeable Tricks and has several Pieces of Painting that reflect no little Honour upon the excellent Artists, by whom they were executed and contrived. Among many others, a Scene of *Covent Garden*, where some Bucks are very happily introduced in a morning Frolick, after the manner of an ingenious Print published a few Years ago, and which cannot but be well recollected by the Public. There are also fine Views of the *Royal Exchange, Westminster Hall, Jonathan's* Coffee-House, and the more public Receptacle for mad People, *Bedlam*. The Contriver or Author of this Pantomime has introduced an Elephant (which walks across the Stage and knocks the Clown down) with the greatest Success: 'Tis perhaps as near Life as Imagination can possibly represent it, and in fact leaves but little or no Applause to the celebrated Ostrich in the *Sorcerer.—Harlequin's* first Appearance in the Moon has a pretty Effect enough, and Hecate's Dress is very well imagined. Upon the whole, 'tis a most agreeable Piece of *Mummery*, and considerably superior to many *Pantomimes* I have seen, where there was much greater Shew, but not half so much Incident or Business.'[20]

So much of Rich's success as director at Covent Garden lay in pantomime that it is not surprising to find that his rival attempted, to a certain extent, to compete with him. Garrick had begun his management at Drury Lane by pouring contempt on the attraction of mere song and spectacle, and in his opening prologue had said:

> 'Tis yours this night to bid the reign commence
> Of rescued nature, and reviving sense;
> To chase the charms of *sound* the pomp of *show*,
> For useful mirth and salutary woe.

But Garrick had to learn the lesson taught by another writer of his day: 'the multitude are incapable of distinguishing; and if their ears are but tickled, and their sight gratified, they re-echo applause, and go away contented; so that [Harlequin]

[20] *The Weekly Amusement*, 24–26 Dec. 1769.

Doctor Faustus, or the Coronation in Harry the Eighth, will bring in a full house very often when Hamlet or Othello might be a losing play.'[21]

He found in Woodward a harlequin who was second only to Rich himself in his mastery of the art of pantomime. Woodward excelled in miming but, as we have seen, he was also a first-class comic actor. This led a critic of *Harlequin Ranger* (1753) to make the interesting suggestion that he should 'appear in the character of a speaking Harlequin, after the manner of the Italian Comedy; and indeed it is not a little surprising that nothing of this kind has yet been admitted upon our stage.'[22] Another thought it was 'a very disagreeable prostitution, for so good a comedian, to be skipping about the stage for an hour or two, without meaning or design.'

In general, Drury Lane pantomimes offered much the same attractions as Covent Garden. The age-old dumb show of the love between Harlequin and Columbine led on to transformation scenes in which, as a Drury Lane actor wrote, palaces and tents became huts and cottages, men and women changed to wheel-barrows and joint stools, colonnades were suddenly beds of tulips, and shops were surpringly serpents and ostriches.[23] Another of its pantomimes, *The Genii*, offered 'An Arabian Night's entertainment' with a last scene that showed 'sumptuous palaces' in a glow of light.[24]

However, Garrick's real attempt to compete with Covent Garden in 'the pomp of show' was better seen in 'entertainments' than in pantomime. They were basically trivial, but were rich in colour and fancy. The German visitor, D'Archenholz,[25] was so struck by them as to give them a fairly full description: 'Among the number of *peculiarities* belonging to the English

21 *A Dialogue in the Shades, between the celebrated Mrs. Cibber, and the no-less celebrated Mrs. Woffington* (1766), pp. 15–16.
22 Quoted in *The London Stage* (ed. Stone), p. 382. Cf. C. W. Beaumont, *The History of Harlequin* (1926), pp. 101–9.
23 Thomas Davies, *Memoirs of David Garrick* (1808), i. 130.
24 Quoted in *The London Stage* (ed. Stone), p. 342.
25 *A Picture of England* (Dublin, 1791), p. 236.

playhouses, may be reckoned the afterpieces called ENTER-TAINMENTS. These for the most part, consist of a happy mixture of dialogue, song, and dance; the decorations are amazing; and the machinery is carried to the most astonishing perfection. The people are uncommonly attached to this kind of diversion. All the great events that occur to the nation are dramatised and represented on the stage; for example, the coronation of the present King; the Prince of Wales receiving the order of the garter; the grand review at Portsmouth in 1774.' He went on to say that they often lasted ninety minutes, and were given after one of Shakespeare's plays.

The 'crowning' mentioned by D'Archenholz had originally been given (at a cost of a thousand pounds) in October 1727 at Drury Lane Theatre, to celebrate the accession of George II, in a performance of *Henry VIII* and 'the coronation of Anne Bullen and the military ceremony of the Champion.'[26] In 1761, both patent houses decided to honour George III in the same way, and on this occasion Rich's production certainly surpassed Garrick's. The actor knew that the harlequin 'had a taste in ordering, dressing, and setting out these pompous processions, superior to his own,'[27] so he resigned himself to defeat in the matter of costume and parade, but hoped to satisfy audiences with a novelty: 'the stage was . . . opened into Drury Lane; and a new and unexpected sight surprised the audience, of a real bonfire, and the populace huzzaing and drinking porter to the health of Queen Anne Bullen.' Unfortunately the smoke from the fire made everyone uncomfortable.

Garrick took more care in presenting the next one, *The Institution of the Knights of the Garter* (1771),[28] and did not stint money for scenery and dresses. The venue was Windsor in time of Edward III, and Garrick's scenario was based on a dramatic poem by Gilbert West. The first scene showed the Knights in their stalls in St. George's Chapel; then the second part

26 John Genest, *An Account of the English Stage* (Bath, 1832), III. 197–209.
27 Thomas Davies, *Memoirs of David Garrick*, i. 365.
28 The installation was of Earl Gower, not the Prince of Wales.

revealed the outside of Windsor Castle. 'A prospect of it afterwards being shewn from within the gate, the grand procession of the Knights to St. George's Hall takes place.' The last part of the ceremony presented the Knights 'feasting in a most sumptuous manner' in the Hall. The piece ended 'with the Genius of England showing him in a vision, the precious fruit the tree shall bear which he has planted in this island; on this Neptune appears, receiving the commands of Britannia, who is seated on the terrestrial globe; the Temple of Victory next arises and the drama concludes with the grand chorus in these words:

> Hail mighty nation, ever fam'd in war.
> Lo, heav'n descends thy festivals to share!
> Celestial bards in living lays shall sing
> Britannia's glories, and her MATCHLESS KING.'

To the relief of the present-day reader, the newspaper reporter adds, 'a number of humorous dialogues are interspersed among the above.'[29]

The scenes for the Garter ceremonies were painted by Carver and John French of the Drury Lane staff, but the set for the grand naval review, mentioned by D'Archenholz, was designed by De Loutherbourg. This entertainment took the form of 'a Grand Occasional Scene' in Arne's *Alfred* (1773).

To D'Archenholz, however, the most remarkable of the 'entertainments' was *The Jubilee*, as given at Drury Lane in 1769. He said, 'When this is acted, the scenes are painted to represent the market-place at Stratford. At a certain signal, the stage is filled with a mob of country people, whom they actually take out of the streets on purpose; and then begins a procession, the like of which has never been seen in any theatre.'[30]

The details of the 'entertainment' may be found in Garrick's own manuscript. The procession began with nine men dancers with tambourines, three Graces, two men 'drest in Old English

---

29 *London Chronicle*, 26–29 October 1771
30 D'Archenholz, *op. cit.*, p. 237.

with Mottos of the Theatre upon rich Standards with proper decorations,' followed by drums and fifes. Then came tableaux of characters from different plays by Shakespeare. *The Tempest*, for example, was represented by a 'Sailor with a banner, Ariel with a wand—raising a Tempest, A Ship in distress, sailing down the stage, Prospero with a wand, Miranda, Caliban with a wooden bottle and two sailors—all drunk!' These groups were succeeded by the Demon of Revenge with a burning Torch, and the Tragic Muse, drawn in a chariot by six furies and attended by Fame, Grief, Pity, Despair, and Madness.[31] D'Archenholz was most impressed by the last scene: 'a superb temple, the altar of which is adorned with the principal subjects mentioned by the poet, depicted in transparent paintings.'

After the failure of the real Stratford celebrations, Garrick's heart was certainly in his London production, and its flamboyant effects achieved considerable popularity. He even revived it for performance in the last six months of his professional career, when the young Mrs. Siddons almost lost her nerve in the part of Venus and was led forward from the throng by Garrick himself.

D'Archenholz does not mention yet another popular entertainment, possibly because this one had no topical significance. It was called *A Christmas Tale* (1774) and was scribbled out by Garrick to give the designer, De Loutherbourg, a real chance to show his powers. It included the following scenes:

A beautiful landskip.
Camilla's magnificent garden—The objects in the garden vary their
  colours.
Soft music plays, the laurel unfolds, and discovers the words VALOR,
  CONSTANCY, and HONOR, in letters of gold
Tycho sounds the horn; it thunders, the rocks split open and discover
  the castle of Nigromant, and the fiery lake.

---

[31] Huntington Library K-D, vol. 332, f. 24 seq. Cf. E. P. Stein, *Three Plays by David Garrick* (New York, 1926), pp. 86, 92.

The seraglio breaks to pieces, and discovers the whole palace in flames.

The flames and ruins of the castle vanish away, and discover a fine moonlight scene.

A fine prospect of the sea, and a castle at a distance, with the sun rising.

Horace Walpole thought only the scenery saved the piece 'from being sent to the devil,' and of these the burning palace was the most admired. It may have owed some of its success to the use of licopodium to suggest a fiery blaze, a device learned from France by Garrick and De Loutherbourg.[32]

Whatever its source, we must remember that exotic scenery was greatly appreciated at this period, and the 'propriety' of the painting even more so. The audience's attitude is well expressed by Roger Pickering: 'If the Streets, Buildings, Rooms and Furniture, Gardens, Views of the Country, etc., be executed in the Taste of the Country where the Scene of the Action in the Play lies, and the *keeping* and *Perspective* be *good*, the whole House never fails to give the most audible Evidence of their Satisfaction' (p. 59).

With the arrival of De Loutherbourg in London late in 1771, a new era in theatre spectacle had begun. For ten years he was associated with Drury Lane Theatre, not as a scene painter so much as a designer of stage effects, supervising scenery, lighting and costume.

He well understood the point of view about lighting expressed earlier by Algarotti in his *Essay on the Opera*:[33] 'What wonderful things might not be produced by the light, when not dispensed in that equal manner, and by degrees, as is now the custom. Were it to be played off with a masterly artifice, distributing it in a strong mass on some parts of the stage, and by depriving others, as it were, at the same time, it is hardly credible what effects might be produced thereby; for instance, a *chiar oscuro*,

32 F. A. Hedgcock, *A Cosmopolitan Actor: David Garrick and his French Friends* (1911), p. 392.

33 Pp. 86–7.

for strength and vivacity, not inferior to that so much admired in the prints of Rembrandt.' Algarotti added that these effects were a serious possibility since they had been achieved without difficulty in miniature theatres in what were called 'mathematical optic-views, that represent sea ports, fleets engaged, etc. Therein the light is admitted through oiled paper, that deadens the rays which might prove too striking, and by that means is so attempered that its various rays gently associate, and are reflected with the greatest harmony.'

In 1782, De Loutherbourg was to give himself up to experiment with the Eidophusikon, a miniature theatre of the kind described; but in the seventies, he displayed his talents at Drury Lane in a number of ways. Of these, the most important was the new method of achieving spectacular lighting effects.

Changes in the lighting of Drury Lane Theatre had taken place after Garrick's return from the Continent in 1765. The chandeliers with their dozen candles apiece were removed, and wing lights were substituted for them. These were of candle or oil—there is a reference to 'spermaceti in the girandoles'[34]—and stood in holders one above the other in a wooden frame. Their power was intensified by the tin reflectors attached to them, and it could be directed either towards or away from the stage. This new control over illumination meant that it was now easy to indicate the waxing or waning of light, at dawn or dusk. De Loutherbourg used this device frequently, but was especially clever at charming audiences through changing the tints of the scenery by throwing light upon it through coloured silk screens. This is what happened when the objects in Camilla's garden varied their colours.

By general agreement De Loutherbourg was held to be a most ingenious designer, but it is not always possible to understand, from the available accounts, exactly what he achieved. In *Alfred*, the ships for the naval review were not painted on the flats, but Domenic Serres, the marine artist, was called in to supply models of the real vessels for employment—in some

34 Huntington Library MS. LA 296, f.19.

undefined but very impressive way—on the set.[35] In *The Critic*, 'the scene of the camp, and the scene of the battle with the Armada, were executed in the most masterly manner. The motion of the sea, and the destruction occasioned by the fire-ships, were happily contrived and accurately represented.'[36] This appears to involve far more than scenery, as does the 'beautiful perspective view of Coxheath camp' exhibited in the musical entertainment called *The Camp*: 'by a kind of magic peculiar to himself, he makes the different battalions, composed of small figures, march out in excellent order, into the front of their lines to the astonishment of every spectator.'[37] The emphasis, as in pantomime, is still on surprise, but it also aims at awe. De Loutherbourg made illusion a fine art, delicately 'attempering' his shades and effects to give his audience a sense of wonder and delight.

By the end of Garrick's life, spectacle was enjoyed for itself alone. This may seem an ironical turn when we think of his avowed contempt for 'the pomp of show', but it must be remembered that painting in general now attracted much public interest and that his scenographers were given the necessary impulse to attain the highest standards.

Naturalism hardly shows itself. Although water had been used for spectacular effects at other theatres earlier in the century, it was not available for them at Drury Lane until the rebuilding of the theatre in 1794. In that year, a versifier noted the change and the earlier practice:

> Behold obedient to the Prompter's Bell
> Our tide shall flow and real water swell,
> No river of meandering paste board made,
> No gentle tinkling of a Tin cascade
> No brook of Broad cloth shall be set in motion,
> Our Ships be wreck'd upon a wooden Ocean.[38]

35 Sybil Rosenfeld and E. Croft-Murray, 'Checklist of Scene Painters', *Theatre Notebook*, xx (1965), 36.
36 *Universal Magazine*, lxv (1779), 229.
37 *Morning Post*, 16 October 1778.
38 Huntington Library MS. LA 2459, f. 19.

As early as 1775, Sheridan had laughed at the tin cascade in the prologue to *St. Patrick's Day*.

In scenery as in costume, standards of what critics called 'propriety' led in the direction of naturalism. Look at the following piece of criticism in the *Morning Chronicle*: 'At Drury Lane whenever they make an apartment, they always lower down a suitable ceiling to it; not so at Covent Garden; for whether they represent a room, hall or inside of a palace, we are obliged to think their house is roofless; as we have always to behold the skies made of plain coloured cloth, which is a very great impropriety. . . . Our correspondent would therefore advise them to get proper sets of ceilings painted.'[39]

This is a pointer to the way in which taste was changing, and when Garrick brought in people from the streets to represent the crowd at Stratford-upon-Avon or found means to show real people in the real street outside Drury Lane Theatre, he anticipated to some degree the development of naturalism in the next century and a half.

[39] 11 Dec. 1774.

CHAPTER FIVE

The Audience

In 1737 the Licensing Act had given the two patent houses a monopoly of theatrical entertainment (other than musical) for the winter season, the period from September to May. Foote calculated that these playhouses attracted very considerable number of people: 'Upon the least favourable Calculation, the numbers of those called Play-Followers, cannot be rated at less than twelve thousand in this Metropolis.'[1] Theophilus Cibber, too, remarked on the rapid growth of audiences at Drury Lane and Covent Garden: 'Would you not acquaint such as may not have consider'd it, that this Metropolis is amazingly encreas'd, that Property is greatly diffus'd; that many Families are advanc'd;—that all Degrees of People go to Plays, as the most rational Amusement;—that there are near thirty times the Number of Spectators there were 30 Years ago;—that six Theatres have flourished in one Season, when there were much fewer Numbers to support them;—and that the Town now have but two to go to.'[2] Since both writers wanted to see more licensed theatres opened, it was in their interest to suggest that there was a greater demand for plays than really existed, but even when we discount some of their enthusiasm, we are still left with large numbers of people who might be rated as

---

1 *A Treatise on the Passions*, p. 3; Cf. *A Letter of Compliment to the Ingenious Author of a Treatise on the Passions*, p. 6.
2 *An Epistle from Theophilus Cibber to David Garrick, Esq;* (1745), p. 25.

keen followers of the drama. We may therefore accept the figure noted by an anonymous letter-writer, who compared the situation in 1770 with that in 1737 and thought that there was 'in every part of London an increase in playgoers in proportion as 20 is to 1.'[3]

It is probably unwise to try to be too precise about the size of the patent houses, but we shall not be far out if we calculate that at the begining of Garrick's management, Drury Lane held twelve hundred people, and that it had increased its capacity by another thousand before he retired. Covent Garden could take about thirteen hundred.[4] Both theatres crammed in more when they had exceptional attractions to offer. The admission charges were one shilling for the upper gallery, two shillings for the gallery, three for the pit, and five for the boxes.

Performance began between six and six-thirty, but the play-houses were open much earlier so that the eager might take a seat. When Boswell wanted to see Garrick as Lear, he found the pit full at ten past four. To get good places for the first perfor-mance of Frances Sheridan's *The Discovery*, he went to Drury Lane at four o'clock with two friends; the pair put their hats on the benches and went away to have dinner, while he kept watch and chatted with Oliver Goldsmith.[5] Sylas Neville attended a performace of *Rule a Wife and have a Wife* at the same house on 7 March 1767, and while he was waiting, was so hemmed in that he could not even read his newspaper. When he went there again, to see *The West Indian*, he could find no room in the pit and had to go to the 'best' gallery.[6]

Footmen were often sent to keep places for their masters. If their betters were late in arriving, the servants sometimes disgusted the ladies and gentlemen sitting around them. One such occasion is reported by 'F.H.' in the *London Chronicle*, 7–9

3 *The Correspondence of King George III*, 1760–83 (ed. Fortescue, 1927), ii. 194–7.
4 H. W. Pedicord, *The Theatrical Public in the Time of Garrick* (New York, 1954), pp. 4–15.
5 *London Journal* (ed. F. A. Pottle, London, 1950), pp. 257, 176.
6 *The Diary of Sylas Neville* (ed. B. Cozens-Hardy, 1950), pp. 5, 119.

November 1769, with a possible remedy: 'By the assistance of
the Box-keeper we found ourselves extremely well seated long
before the curtain drew up; but how were we surprised, as soon
as the candles began to be lighted, to find one of our company,
a Lady of the first fashion, planted between two very ordinary
looking fellows, one of whom we soon discovered, from his
livery, to what order he belonged: the other, from his dress,
seemed to be of much meaner rank, and was probably one of
those people whom the house provides to keep places when the
footman can't be spared, or the party is, perhaps unprovided at
home with such a kind of utensil. Mortified as we were at the
Lady's disagreeable situation, we used every means in our
power to remove these very uncouth neighbours, but in vain,
and the third act was well nigh finished, before the Gentlemen
arrived whose places these Gentry had so long occupied. This,
Mr. Printer, is no imaginary grievance . . . but calls aloud for
redress, and has indeed been long complained of.—As I am
lately returned from a tour in foreign parts, I would humbly
propose to the managers of both theatres to adopt the plan of
their neighbours on the continent, and follow the example set
them by their fellow-labourers abroad, where this part of the
œconomy of the stage is conducted with the greatest delicacy, by
the following easy, simple method; viz. only writing the names
of the persons who bespeak their places, on pieces of paper, and
affixing them to their respective seats, by which means the
greatest order and decorum will be established, and the house
cleared of this insufferable nuisance.' The suggestion was not
accepted, and the footmen keeping places went on irritating the
ladies and gentlemen who sat next to them.

To the eighteenth century God had made men high or lowly
and ordered their estate even in the playhouse; by common
consent, certain parts of the theatre properly belonged to
certain sorts of people. Footmen (after keeping places below)
and sailors were to be found in the upper gallery; tradespeople
went into the 'best' gallery; the professional classes sat in the
pit, and the aristocracy in the boxes. These were general rules

but they were not always applied. Criminals also knew their stations: pickpockets were everywhere but throve most in the crowded entrance passages. Prostitutes of both sexes were to be found at the back of the front boxes[7] as well as in the galleries and the front rows of the green boxes.

The characteristics of the various sections in the theatre are interestingly described in Garrick's epilogue[8] to Henry Crisp's *Virginia*:

> [*To Upper Gallery*] The twelve-pence seat you there,
> so near the ceiling,
> The folks below can't boast a better feeling.
> No high-bred prud'ry in your region lurks,
> You boldly laugh and cry, as Nature works.
> . . . .
> Some Maiden Dames, who hold the Middle Floor
> (*Middle Gallery*)
> And fly from naughty man at forty-four;
> With turn'd up eyes, applaud Virginia's scape,
> And now they'd do the same to shun a rape;
> So very chaste, they live in constant fears,
> And apprehension strengthens with their years.
> Ye Bucks, who from the Pit your terrors send,
> Yet love distressed damsels to befriend;
> You think this tragic joke too far was carried;
> And wish, to set all right, the maid had married.
> . . .
> May I approach unto the Boxes, pray—
> And there search out a judgment on the Play?
> In vain, alas! I should attempt to find it—
> Fine Ladies see a Play, but never mind it—
> 'Tis vulgar to be mov'd by acted passion,
> Or form opinions, 'till they're fixed by fashion.

D'Archenholz noted that actors paid rather more attention to the galleries than to the boxes, and this was probably because

7 *London Chronicle*, 17–20 September, 1785; *The Monitor* (1767), 14 Nov. 1767.
8 Folger Library MS. W. b. 467, f. 36.

of their readier response, a willingness to show their feelings without fear.[9] *The Rational Rosciad* described their favourite forms of entertainment:

> Dear pantomime can raise their spirits high,
> And lift their souls, on pullies to the sky;
> A drunken sailor, or a smutty jest,
> Or gay infernal in hell fashion drest,
> Are things, from which they endless pleasure quaff,
> For nothing pleases, but makes them laugh.[10]

They also aired their opinions frankly, and Goldsmith's citizen of the world complained that 'those who were undermost all the day, now enjoyed a temporary eminence, and became masters of the ceremonies. It was they who called for the music, indulging every noisy freedom, and testifying all the insolence of beggars in exaltation.'[11] The author of *Reflections upon Theatrical Expression in Tragedy* confirmed this: 'What interrupting Insolence do we meet from the Galleries almost during the whole Performance! Insolence that nothing but the *Military* and *Peace-Officer* can correct.'[12] The Welsh footmen were noted for being particularly turbulent.[13]

Physical conditions in the upper gallery were enough to make anyone irritable. Boswell scrambled into it on a night when Garrick played Bayes in *The Rehearsal* and found the heat from all the bodies pressed together unbearable.[14] Though everyone was laughing, he himself could see and hear little of what was going on. Sylas Neville was 'almost stewed'.[15]

When the 'gods' were offended, everyone felt the force of their displeasure. Ammunition was near at hand, as may be noted from a manuscript version of Garrick's *Peep behind the Curtain*.[16] The theatre housekeeper orders the sweeper to 'be sure you take

9 P. 238.
10 (1767), p. 15.
11 Letter XXI.
12 (1755), p. 78.
13 J. P. Malcolm, *Anecdotes of the Manners and Customs of London during the Eighteenth Century* (1808), p. 358.
14 *Boswell for the Defence* (London, 1960), p. 68.
15 *Op. cit.*, p. 119.
16 Huntington Library MS. LA 271.

away all the Chew'd Apples, Orange Peel and Walnut Shells you find in the upper Gallery.' The sweeping woman replies, 'I believe they eat more of that trash there than in all London besides.' Much of it rained on the stage and pit when the upper gallery grew angry. One such occasion is described by Neville: in a patriotic fury the gods called for 'The Roast beef of Old England' to be played at the beginning, and between the acts of Macklin's *Love à la Mode*. Their demand was refused, so they showered orange peel on the stage. In December 1762, when public feeling was high against Bute and all Scots, two Highland officers entered the pit at Covent Garden only to be greeted with hisses and yells of 'No Scots! No Scots! Out with them!' from an outraged upper gallery that pelted them with apples.[17] Members of the audience were fair game, but the theatres took strong objection to the harassing of performers. In fact, the management of Drury Lane inserted a notice in the *Public Advertiser* of 13 November 1776, saying that twenty guineas reward would be paid to every person securing a conviction of anyone throwing apples and oranges at the actors.

The wilder spirits needed to show their strong emotions by throwing something heavier. When a 'villain' threw a glass bottle from the upper gallery of Covent Garden Theatre into the orchestra, he did not hurt anyone, but the *London Chronicle* remarked, 'offences of this kind, which have been too frequent of late, ought to be severely punished.'[18] The prize attempt occurred in the same theatre, when a man sitting in the sixth row of the upper gallery

threw a keg (which he had brought full of liquor into the house) over the gallery front. It fell upon a lady's head, who sat in that part of the pit that was railed into boxes, but the lady's hair being dressed in high *ton* the artificial mountain luckily prevented the mischief that otherwise might have been occasioned ...The fellow was carried to the Public-office in Bow-street, and then committed to Tothill fields Bridewell.[19]

17 Boswell, *London Journal* (ed. cit.,) pp. 71–2.
18 14–16 January 1772.   19 *Chester Chronicle*, 7 March 1776.

G

By contrast, the inhabitants of the other (sometimes distinguished as 'the middle' or 'best') gallery were of a quiet temper. *The Rational Rosciad*, again, specifies its characteristics:

> In the mid station, solidly sedate,
> The well fed tradesman sits, in drowsy state;
> In vain may real wit be spoke with grace,
> He still retains his gravity of face;
> But maxims prudent and proverbial phrase,
> Make him grin horrible, with ha! ha! gaze.
> Twelve times twelve's a hundred and forty four,
> Will set the middle gallery in a roar;
> Method and business, never fail to charm.

The 'citizen of the world' found that they were 'not so riotous as those above them, nor yet so tame as those below' and that they spent their time waiting for the play to begin by quietly 'eating oranges, reading the story of the play, or making assignations.'[20]

The last of these activities was a commonplace one in the theatres of the day but has seldom been associated, by later commentators, with the bourgeois. Yet as far back as the preface to *The Twin Rivals* (1702), Farquhar had quoted one city man as saying, 'however pious we may appear to be at home, yet we never go to that end of the town but with an intention to be lewd.' In other words, once they were in the more fashionable quarter they imitated their betters, a point also made in a piece of dialogue in Macklin's manuscript satire, *Covent Garden Theatre* (1752):

Marforio: Well, if you must be satyrical, confine your Satyr to the City.
Pasquin: No, I'll begin at the Source—the Bourgoie is but the Ape of the Courtier; Correct the one, other Mends of course.[21]

Nevertheless the point of view put forward by the author of *The Rational Rosciad* had its merits: by common convention the merchant classes did not appreciate the subtle or the bawdy and

20 Letter XXI.   21 Huntington Library MS. LA 96, f. 6.

were anxious to preserve appearances. They differed from the aristocracy in delighting in plays that had a background in trade: for example, one writer noted that 'among us are never to be seen the same brilliant audiences for *George Barnwell* as at the *Distrest Mother*.'

The pit considered itself the court of critical jurisdiction,[22] and its lively nature appears in another summary from *The Rational Rosciad*:

> The educated gentry in the pit
> Require correctness, repartee, and wit.

Successful and unsuccessful authors, gentlemen of the town, and professional men made up a large part of its numbers. Lawyers were especially prominent. The Abbé Le Blanc mentioned that 'most of them live in colleges [inns of court], where conversing always with one another, they mutually preserve a spirit of independence thro' the body, and with great ease form cabals. These gentlemen, in the stage entertainments of London, behave much like our foot-boys, in those at a [French] fair. . . . At Paris, the cabals of the pit are only among young fellows, whose years may excuse their folly, or persons of the meanest education and stamp: here they are the fruit of deliberations in a very grave body of people, who are not less formidable to the minister in place, than to the theatrical writers.'[23] Four years later, the author of *The Theatrical Manager* made similar charges against lawyers' clerks, who 'seem to claim, or rather demand, a Prerogative in judging all kinds of Writings, and handle an Author as rude as an Old Bailey Jury does a Criminal; condemn him to death, without considering whether he deserves it.'[24]

Perceptively, Goldsmith tells us that the people in the pit 'were assembled partly to be amused, and partly to shew their taste; appearing to labour under that restraint which an

22 See D. F. Smith, *The Critics in the Audience* (Albuquerque, 1953), *passim*.

23 *Op. cit.*, ii. 314.   24 (1751), p. v.   91

affectation of superior discernment generally produces. My companion, however, informed me that not one in an hundred of them knew even the first principles of criticism; that they assumed the right of being censors, because there was no one to contradict their pretensions.'[25]

The uneducated gentry seem to have been quite unrestrained, as is evident in Macklin's satirical picture of Sir Roger Ringwood, 'a five bottle man . . . remarkable for his Taste in dramatic Performances, and the loudest Voice that ever damn'd a Play.' His demands were simple: 'be it tragedy or farce I don't care a Hare's Scut, so there is Fun in it. . . . But if it is any of your New Moral Stuff, according to Rule, I shall Tip it dead Hollow[26] (*Hollows*).'[27] Another writer described the breed more pithily:

> Blockheads and *Bloods* in Pit and Boxes roar,
> Support a Pantomime and damn a *Moore;*
> Arraign the traitor Garrick's insolence,
> Who dar'd to satirise the want of Sense.[28]

The boxes were held to be places where, like Lord Foppington earlier, people might 'make a figure in a side-box, and entertain themselves with looking upon the company.' Many of the wealthiest and most fashionable men and women occupied them, conscious that they were the centres of attention. Once again Goldsmith's citizen of the world furnishes an apt comment on their appearance: 'The rest of the audience came merely for their own amusement; these rather to furnish out part of an entertainment themselves. I could not avoid considering them as acting parts in dumb-shew; not a courtesy or a nod that was not the result of art; not a look nor a smile that was not designed for murder. Gentlemen and ladies ogled each other through spectacles.' Another writer describes 'Lady Peacock', who sought a front box but had to be content with the balcony: 'she'll take it rather than stay away;—the LIGHTS,

25 *The Citizen of the World*, Letter XXI.   26 Halloo.
27 Huntington Library MS. LA 96, p. 28; cf. D. F. Smith, *op cit.*, p. 91.
28 [W. Kenrick], *The Pasquinade* (1753), p. 17.

you know,—and GLARE, and—all that tickles their Vanity—
they'd as lief be damn'd as not seen.'[29] Yet there were occasions
when some ladies found it best to steal away to the gallery, to
enjoy some risqué jokes that they would have had to ignore were
they in full view of the audience:

> My lady *Prim* who makes a mighty pother
> Has buried Husbands three, and weds another,
> Cries, Lord!—I would not for the world be seen
> At Congreve's Plays, so shameful, so unclean!—
> Yet in the Gallery with her maid undress'd,
> Close and Incog: she sits a greedy Guest;
> Takes Snuff, and Smacks her Lips, at ev'ry Sav'ry jest.[30]

Lady Prim and her kind do not appear, however, to have been
typical of aristocratic patrons of the drama, and there is good
reason to believe that by the end of the period we are discussing,
the nobility in general attended the playhouses far less frequently than had been the case earlier. R. B. Sheridan, as
manager of Drury Lane, went into the question in 1777, and
concluded that the 'Politer Streets' were now at some distance
from the patent theatres, and that ladies had genuine difficulty
in reaching their carriages and chairs. There were other
causes, too, of the falling away: anyone who lived at an even
greater distance, or had to attend parliament, or even to dine
at the fashionable, later hour, found it impossible to reach the
playhouse by half-past six, and was lucky to be there before the
performances were half over.[31] Consequently Sheridan put
forward a proposal that a third theatre should be erected on a
subscription basis and that, to suit its noble patrons, it should be
small, and its programmes should start at a comparatively late
hour. Nothing came of the suggestion, but it is significant in
itself.

The most troublesome people in the theatre were the 'bucks',
who defied convention by taking up their seats wherever they

29 *Brief Remarks on the Original and Present State of the Drama* (1758), p. 28.
30 Prologue by Garrick now Huntington Library MS. LA 419.
31 *Letters of R. B. Sheridan* (ed. C. Price, Oxford, 1966), i. 117–19.   93

felt disposed to go. A most vivid description of them appears in an epilogue spoken by Thomas King, on 29 April 1760:

. . .

If warm'd to Praise, you eccho our renown
Or urg'd to Fury, tear our Benches down,
Is still the same—To one bright Goal ye haste
To shew your Spirit and approve your Taste.
'Tis not in Nature for you to be quiet,
No—damme!—Bucks exist but in a Riot.
   For Instance, now—to charm th' admiring Croud
Your Bucks i' th' Boxes sneer and talk aloud.
Thence to the more commodious Seat they run
                         [Points to the Upper Boxes]
(Illo! Illo! my Bucks! well, what's the Fun?)
Tho' Shakespeare speaks, regardless of the Play,
They loll and laugh the sprightly hours away
For to seem sensible of real Merit,
Is certainly—*beneath us Lads of Spirit,*
   Your Bucks i' th' Pit are—Miracles of Learning!
Who point out Faults to shew their own discerning.
And Giant-like, bestriding martyr'd Sense,
Proclaim their Genius and—*vast Consequence.*
   The middle Row, whose keener views of Bliss
                       [Points to the Middle Gallery]
Are chiefly centr'd in a fav'rite Miss;
A set of jovial Bucks who there resort,
Flush'd from the Tavern—reeling ripe for Sport—
Whisp'ring soft Nonsense in the Fair One's Ear,
And wholly ignorant what passes here.

. . .

High over all, supremely wise are they   *[Upper*
Who Insects-like, together swarm, to prey   *Gallery]*
On the fresh Carcase of the newborn Play
In various kinds of Fun, their Hours they chase
Careless alike of Action, Time, or Place.
Some the shrill Trumpet, some the Cat-call try
Some Broomstickado's[32] softer Harmony.

[32] A character in Christopher Smart's *Old Woman's Oratory*, who seems

Others in nobler Mimickry excell,
You'd think 'em Beasts, they act the Beast so well.
Here mews a Cat—there barks a snarling Dog—
Here crows a Cock—there grunts a bristled Hog.
'Tir'd with the Noise, some rusticated Clown,
Roars from his empty Stomach—knock him down!
Here Nosey, Nosey, merry Witlings cry—
There Taylors! Taylors! ecchoing Smarts reply—
'Till mingled Shouts and Screams pierce thro' the
vaulted Sky.[33]

We have only to recall Boswell's delight in having entertained the Covent Garden audience by lowing like a cow,[34] to see that this description of the bucks is by no means exaggerated.

They were particularly fond of sitting on the stage and though this pleasure was not confined to them, they provided much of the resistance to Garrick's attempts to keep members of the audience on the other side of the proscenium. The author of *The D--ry L-ne P--yh--se Broke Open*[35] noted that they 'pop in and out with as little Opposition as Modesty; and have made so absolute a Burrow of the Stage, that unless they are *ferreted* out by some Means or other, we may bid farewell to Theatrical Entertainments.' The writer adds, 'I hope it is not the Consideration of their paying something more behind the Scenes, that induces you to admit 'em; for take my Word, in the End, you will be a great Loser by this most intollerable Innovation.'

In the winter of 1748, Garrick made an unsuccessful effort to stop people crowding upon the stage. A year later he added to his *Lethe* a passage describing 'a fine gentleman' who proudly describes his behaviour at the playhouse: 'I dress in the Evening, and go generally behind the Scenes of both Playhouses; not . . . to be diverted with the Play, but to intrigue, and shew myself—I stand upon the Stage, talk loud, and stare about—which confounds the Actors, and disturbs the Audience;

to have pretended to play on a broomstick: see *The London Stage* (ed. Stone), pp. 314, 672,

33 Huntington Library MS. LA 175.
34 *London Journal, ed. cit.,* p. 236, n. 1.   35 (1748), p. 18.

upon which the Galleries, who hate the Appearance of one of us, begin to *hiss*, and cry *off, off*, while I undaunted, stamp my Foot so—loll with my Shoulder thus—take Snuff with my Right-hand, and smile scornfully—thus—This exasperates the Savages, and they attack us with Vollies of suck'd Oranges, and half eaten Pippins.'[36]

A satire was not enough to put an end to the nuisance, and more resolute methods had to be adopted. Some of the trouble was caused by the building, on benefit nights, of tiers of seats at the back of the stage and the placing of benches in front of the stage boxes. The actors agreed to this because it meant a considerable increase in the profits of their nights, but they were also the first to suffer from its inconveniences. They were greatly impeded in their action: for example, a player who had to escape over a balcony also had to push his way through the people sitting in front of it and apologise as he went along,[37] a practice that put an end to stage illusion for some minutes.

The 'ampitheatre' (as the tiers were called) was finally abandoned by Garrick in 1762, when he increased the seating of the Drury Lane auditorium itself. He announced the innovation in the *Public Advertiser*, 21 February 1763,[38] and noted in passing that there had often been complaints of 'interruptions in the performances occasioned by a crowded stage.' In the next month, his example was followed by the Covent Garden manager, John Beard. It did not entirely end the practice of spectators appearing behind the scenes, and a new effort in this direction was made in September 1776, when Sheridan took over the management at Drury Lane. The *Morning Chronicle*[39] reported: 'Many frequenters of the theatres congratulate the managers on the additional decorum their exhibitions receive by the excluding the parties from behind the scenes. Last season at Drury-Lane so many actresses' sisters, authors, authors' wives, and their wives' friends were

[36] Quoted by D. F. Smith, *op cit.*, p. 75.
[37] P. Fitzgerald, *Life of David Garrick* (1868) ii. 22–4.
[38] *The London Stage*, p. 979.   [39] 30 September 1776.

THE AUDIENCE

admitted, as totally destroyed the delusion [*sic*], intended to be excited by the scenery. Some of the gentlemen from a vanity of having the town think they were in the cabinet of Roscius, thrust themselves so forward on the stage as to offend and disgust the audience entirely.'

It was not difficult to offend the audience and, in the middle years of the century, dissension between rival factions or management and audience reached a pitch of fury that had a parallel outside the theatre only in the excesses of the mob. The most famous of the theatre riots was connected with Garrick's production of *The Chinese Festival*. The manager had engaged the choreographer, Jean Georges Noverre and his company on a one-year contract, and they opened at Drury Lane on 8 November 1755, with fine scenery and costumes as well as a spectacular procession of ninety people. The King's presence at the first performance prevented real disorder, but some voices were heard to cry 'No French dancers.' When the ballet was presented again on 12 November, there was considerable rowdiness. According to a pamphlet called *The Dancers Damn'd*,[40] uproar began at once: 'my brother *Gods* chose to shew their loyalty by stopping the music that was intended for the evening, and calling for *God Save the King, Britain* [*sic*] *strike Home*, [*Rule*] *Britannia*, etc.' When the play was over and the Chinese scenery was brought out, 'the Leader of the loyal party advanced to the front of the gallery' and told the audience that the dancers were foreign dogs who had come to undermine the British constitution. Reason might have suggested what Garrick had already advertised: that since Noverre was a Swiss protestant and there were only very few French members of the company, patriotic feeling need not be excited. The gallery was, however, only in a mood to reply 'Swiss! What the devil do we know of *Swiss!*—a *Swiss* is a foreigner, and all *foreigners* are *Frenchmen*; and so damn you all.' A man was thrown out of the gallery, and military men in the boxes descended into the pit and beat some of its noisy members and thrust them out of the house. The

[40] Pp. 4–7.

ballet was completed to loud applause.[41] On succeeding nights, the gentlemen of the boxes kept order when they were able to be present, and when not, the galleries hooted, broke the chandeliers, and smashed the benches before hurling them into the pit. At the final performance (fifteenth), both sides came ready for battle. Dried peas and tintacks were thrown on to the stage to prevent any dancing, and the playhouse was given up to the struggle. Though the magistrates and constables were called, the conduct of the rioters was so furious that Garrick thought it wiser to dispense with the services of the dancers rather than face any more trouble and damage.

Another riot was caused by the half-price system. Garrick had enlarged the auditorium to accommodate spectators who had formerly sat in the 'ampitheatre'. He then decided to increase his takings by ending the practice by which only half the normal charges for admission were levied on anyone who entered at the end of the third act of the main item in the programme. Since many of the 'afterpieces' attracted crowds quite as often as the opening tragedy or comedy, the new move was resented. Consequently, as a contemporary observed, 'the city bloods imagined that it was an imposition to make them pay full price for old representations, and before they could bring the managers of both houses to what they thought a right way of thinking, they did more injury, by tearing up benches, breaking up scenes and chandeliers, and the like than the profits amounted to for a whole season.[42] It took two nights' disturbances[43] to force Garrick to restore half-price for all performances, except those of the first season of a new, expensive pantomime.

When full prices were charged for the opera *Artaxerxes* at Covent Garden on 24 February, the audience behaved even more violently. Box linings were ripped, benches and girandoles smashed, and an attempt was even made to break down the

---

41 F. A. Hedgcock, . . . *David Garrick and his French Friends* (1911) pp. 131–4, quoting from the *Journal Étranger*, December 1755, p. 233.

42 *A Dialogue in the Shades*, p. 16.   43 25 and 26 January 1763.

wooden pillars holding up the galleries. The manager defended himself by saying that for *Artaxerxes* the expenses of performance were much higher than usual, and that he would refuse demands that were 'enforced by means subversive to Private Property, and in violation of that decorum which is due to all public assemblies,'[44] but his words had no effect. He had to yield, though he took the opportunity of pointing out that theatrical entertainments were now twice as costly as they had been forty years ago.

An audience's sudden anger was never better demonstrated than at the third night of Bate's *The Blackamoor Wash'd White* (1776). Some hissing had been heard at the first and second performances, but at the third, real fury was shown: 'Several of the exceptionable passages were omitted but some gentlemen in the boxes shewed their disappointment in a very vociferous manner, which was so resented by the rest of the house, that an universal uproar ensued, and those who attacked the piece were saluted with volleys of oranges and apples, and even halfpence; numbers of the audience at length got upon the stage; several persons were knocked down, and many turned out of the house. A man was thrown from the gallery, but saved himself from hurt by hanging on the chandelier; and a lady of high rank was struck in the face with an orange. In short, the whole scene was more alarming than any one that has occurred on such an occasion.'[45] At the fourth performance, the opponents of the piece assembled in full force and, though Garrick pleaded with them several times, they were not satisfied till one of the actors came and reported that Bate had taken possession of the copy of the play and left the theatre. Peace was restored in this way: the rioters' wishes had been obeyed.

Audiences had a high sense of their own dignity, even when their behaviour was far from dignified. When Elizabeth Griffiths's *A Wife in the Right* was presented in March 1772 after a postponement, Shuter was hissed and called upon to apologise

---

44 Quoted from the *Public Advertiser*, in *The London Stage*, p. 980.
45 *Chester Chronicle*, 12 February 1776.

because he was understood to have caused the delay. He then told the audience that he had been suddenly taken ill, but admitted that he had been 'drunk three days before . . . and asked pardon for it.' This was reluctantly granted, but when the play itself came up for judgement, the audience grew irritable at the management's insistence that it should be performed again next evening. So they smashed the lamps, and the play was withdrawn immediately.[46]

When Macklin gave a new interpretation of Macbeth at Covent Garden in October 1773, he thought from the behaviour of some people in the playhouse that there was a plot against him to deprive him of his livelihood. His reaction was so strong that it forfeited sympathy, and even though he gave up playing Macbeth and returned to his old part, Shylock, the audience was irritated by him and the manager thought it best to dismiss him at once. Consequently Macklin took his case to court and moved against his persecutors 'for hissing and otherwise insulting him.' The motion was rejected in the King's Bench on the ground that 'the audience had a right to applaud, condemn, nay, reject, what performers they thought proper.'[47] In other words, the Drama's patrons gave not only its laws but an actor's living, or as Dr. Johnson phrased it, 'we that live to please, must please, to live.' Players were His Majesty's servants, but they were also the public's.

The actors had to submit, but they chafed at their bondage. Macklin had his revenge by obtaining a court order against his tormentors for combining to deprive him of his professional prospects. Others were not so lucky or so resolute.[48] Kitty Clive wrote to Garrick on one occasion to say, 'I hope the theatre will never be in the power of such wretches, who would wish to interrupt every new piece for the honour of having themselves thought judges.'[49] The wish was a vain one whenever the majority of the audience agreed with the 'wretches'.

46 *London Chronicle*, 9–10 March 1772.
47 *Annual Register* (1774), p. 90.   48 *Ibid.*, pp. 118–27.
49 Folger Shakespeare Library MS. Y. c. 552 (1), Nov yᵉ 11. 1767.

Yet it would be a mistake to think that the theatres were often tumultuous. Riots were the more striking because they happened so seldom. In fact, a German visitor thought the English playhouses were far more orderly than those of France or Italy, and was impressed by the quiet attention of the audiences and their not applauding until the actor paused.[50]

Even when an audience was peppery, an actress might restore it to good humour with some blandishments, or some old favourite cool tempers with a jest. An amusing example of this occured in 1775, and concerned the comedian Weston, who was noted for his phlegm:

At the conclusion of the opera of *The Rival Candidates*, the house calling loudly for the epilogue, and Mr. Weston and Dragon not immediately coming on, a ruffian in the upper gallery threw a glass bottle with great fury on the stage, which alarmed several ladies of distinction in the stage boxes:—Weston, however, at his entrance, humorously took advantage of the circumstance; for in the couplet, where he addresses himself to his dog—
What say you, *Dragon*, why's your tail so low?
Be not chop-fall'n, they can't *damn* you, you know.
He gave the last line this turn:
They won't throw *bottles* at your head you know.
It had its desired effect; for the ready and droll application gained him universal applause.

The players were naturally 'chop-fall'n' on nights when the audience was irascible, but were wise to obey its wishes, for its sense of power had increased with the growth in the size of the playhouses. Ready submission was the managers' wisest course too, for once moods of ill-temper were dispelled, they were usually followed by long periods of delighted appreciation.

[50] J. A. Kelly, *German Visitors to English Theaters in the Eighteenth Century* (Princeton, 1936), p. 31.

CHAPTER SIX

Opera and Ballet

A writer in the *London Chronicle* of 11–14 November 1758 declared that Italian opera had not flourished in England until *Arsinoe, Queen of Cyprus* was performed at Drury Lane Theatre on 16 January 1705:

> After having blundered for a great while from one absurdity to another, we were at last convinced that we knew nothing about the matter by a piece called *Arsinoe*. Now the Public began to disrelish what they had hitherto swallowed so eagerly; they plainly perceived that Purcell's preposterous gallimaufries, called Dramatic Operas, were as inferior to *Arsinoe*, as the most dissonant band of parish boys could be to the best regulated and well finished choir. Upon a due consideration therefore of the merits of both sides, the former, after a fair hearing, was dismissed, and rendered incapable. While the *Drama per Musica* was entered upon the list of public places, and from that time to this hath been regarded accordingly.

English performers using both English and Italian appeared in *Arsinoe*, but very soon afterwards opera was given wholly in Italian, generally by Italian singers. It became a very fashionable entertainment, and was strongly supported by the nobility in subscription seasons. The programmes were made up of some thirty-six operas by Handel, including the last unsuccessful one, *Deidamia*, performed in 1741, the year of Garrick's London début.

From that year onwards, Handel devoted much of his energy

to oratorio, and the history of dramatic music in the Garrick period divides itself roughly into Italian opera given at the King's Theatre, and English opera, oratorio, and ballad opera, performed at the patent theatres.

Italian opera at the King's Theatre was managed between 1741 and 1748 by Lord Middlesex, afterwards second Duke of Dorset. He appointed Galuppi as his resident composer, Francesco Vanneschi (the librettist) as stage manager, and Ameconi as designer of scenes. The operas were usually presented on Tuesdays and Saturdays: fifty-six performances were given between 31 October 1741 and 1 June 1742, and forty-eight in the next season, 2 November to 17 May. Almost two-thirds of the total were of works by (or compiled by) Galuppi, and this preponderance was justified, in Burney's words, by the fact that 'many of the refinements in modern melody and effects in dramatic music seem to originate from the genius of Galuppi.' Gluck's *Artaserse* was produced under the title of *Mandane*. Porpora's *Temistocle* drew another note from Burney: 'I never saw Music in which shakes were so lavished: Porpora seemes to have composed the air, "Contrasto assai", in a shivering fit.'[1]

Subscribers were admitted with a silver ticket for the first fifty performances, but in the first season, had to pay extra for the other six. In general, tickets were at half a guinea each, or for the gallery, five shillings. Both charges were sufficiently expensive to keep out all but the well-to-do, though enough money was never available to pay the full expenses of a season. By May 1743, Horace Walpole reported that Lord Middlesex was likely to ruin his family by his extravagance in supporting the opera. 'Besides what he will lose this year, he has not paid his share in the losses of the last, and yet is singly undertaking another for next season, with the almost certainty of losing between four and five thousand pounds, to which the deficiencies

---

1 C. Burney, *A General History of Music* (ed. Mercer, New York, 1935; repr. 1957), ii. 842.

of the opera generally amount now.'² By 14 August, Walpole was exasperated to find that some of the losses would fall upon the subscribers too: 'We were thirty subscribers at two hundred pounds each, which was to last four years, and no other demands ever to be made. Instead of that, we have been made to pay fifty-six pounds over and above the subscription in one winter. I told the Secretary in a passion, that it was the last money I would ever pay for the folly of the directors.'³

The directors might have argued that the subscribers expected too much for their money and that the better the singers were the more the productions would cost; but the enthusiasm of Lord Middlesex did not wane and he continued to meet part of the deficit himself. In the 1743–4 season, Lampugnani became resident composer, and five operas (three of them by him) were given in fifty-four performances. Some attempt was made to attract a wider audience when the Scots song, 'The lass of Patie's mill', was inserted into *Roselinda*. Burney noted, 'as few of the North Britons, or admirers of this national and natural Music, frequent the opera, or mean to give half a guinea to hear a Scots tune, which perhaps their cook-maid Peggy can sing better than any foreigner, this expedient failed of its intended effect.'⁴ No operas were given in the following season, and in 1746 a late start was made because of the troublesome Jacobite rebellion. At the end of that year, Walpole reported: 'We have operas, but no company at them; the Prince [of Wales] and Lord Middlesex *Impressarii*. Plays only are in fashion'⁵ In the season of 1747–8, just twenty-seven performances were given. The subventions of Lord Middlesex came to an end, and retrenchment became necessary. The Abbé Le Blanc came to the conclusion that 'the English, who regard the opera only as a concert, will no longer have any but

---

2 *Letters to Horace Walpole, Earl of Orford to Sir Horace Mann* (1833), i. 311–12.

3 *Ibid.*, i. 349–50.

4 Burney, *ed. cit.*, ii. 843.

5 *Letters . . . of Sir Horace Mann, ed. cit.*, ii. 265.

those that are the least expensive, and in which dresses and decorations may be dispensed with.'[6]

To try to win new support, a company of singers in burletta or comic opera was brought from Italy in November 1748, and comic opera often became a part of the repertory of future seasons. Yet managers still found it hard to pay expenses, and Crosa (in 1750) and Vanneschi (in 1756) had to go abroad to escape their many creditors.

Between 11 November 1758 and 11 June 1763, performances were given under the direction of the leading singer, Colomba Mattei, and her husband, Trombetta. The splendid scenery used in *Attalo* on the first of these nights has already been described,[7] and the first season was also notable for the appearance of Tenducci, who was to delight English opera-goers and concert audiences for many years. The attractions of the second season were considerably fewer, and were to be found chiefly in Mattei's singing and Cornacini's acting. An illuminating review of their performances was written by Oliver Goldsmith for *The Bee*: 'at present, the house seems deserted, the castrati sing to empty benches. . . . To say the truth, the opera, as it is conducted among us, is but a very humdrum amusement; in other countries, the decorations are entirely magnificent, the singers all excellent, and the burletta or interludes, quite entertaining; the best poets compose the words, and the best masters the music, but with us it is otherwise; the decorations are but trifling and cheap; the singers, Mattei only excepted, but indifferent. . . . When such is the case, it is not much to be wondered, if the opera is pretty much neglected; the lower orders of people have neither taste nor fortune to relish such an entertainment; they would find more satisfaction in the *Roast Beef of Old England*, than in the finest closes of an eunuch, they sleep amidst all the agony of a recitative: On the other hand, people of fortune or taste, can hardly be pleased when there is a visible poverty in the decorations, and

---

6 *Letters on the English and French Nations* (1747), ii. 195.
7 See pp. 63–4 above.

H

an entire want of taste in the composition.' He went on to
argue that Metastasio's work was universally admired and
'would alone be sufficient to fill an house.'

He was particularly severe on singers who were not content
with their parts but wanted to insert their favourite airs into
an opera. 'Such songs are generally chosen as surprize rather
than please, where the performer may shew his compass, his
breath, and his volubility. From hence proceed those unnatural
startings, those unmusical closings, and shakes lengthened out
to a painful continuance; such, indeed, may shew a voice, but
it must give a truly delicate ear the utmost uneasiness.' Mattei
did not use trills: she was 'at once both a perfect actress and a
very fine singer.' Goldsmith ended his essay by wondering if
Italian operas would continue to be given in England, because
they seemed 'entirely exotic'.[8] The adjective carries us on to Dr.
Johnson's celebrated description of Italian opera at the end of
our period: 'an exotick and irrational entertainment, which has
been always combated, and always has prevailed.'[9]

It was attacked chiefly because it was sung by Italians in
Italian. Le Blanc enquired: 'Is it surprising that the English are
grown tired of the Italian opera? Three-quarters of the
spectators did not comprehend what was sung, and it was
natural for Farinelli himself to set them yawning when he
passed from air to recitative.'[10] Too often people went to the
opera house because that was the proper thing to do. Sheridan
laughs at this in the words he put into the mouth of Lord
Foppington:

Foppington: Naw, if I find it a good day, I resalve to take the exercise
of riding, so drink my chocolate, and draw on my boots by two.
On my return, I dress; and after dinner, lounge perhaps to the
Opera.
Berinthia: Your lordship, I suppose, is fond of music?
Foppington: O, passionately, on Tuesdays and Saturdays, provided

8 *Collected Works* (ed. Friedman, Oxford 1966), i. 506–8.
9 *Lives of the English Poets* (ed. G. B. Hill, Oxford, 1905), ii. 160.
10 P. 192.

there is good company, and one is not expected to undergo the fatigue of listening.

Amanda: Does your lordship think that the case at the Opera?

Foppington: Most certainly, madam: there is my Lady Tattle, my Lady Prate, my Lady Titter, my Lady Sneer, my Lady Giggle, and my Lady Grin—these have boxes in the front, and while any favourite air is singing, are the prettiest company in the waurld, stap my vitals! Mayn't we hope for the honour to see you added to our society, Madam?

Amanda: Alas, my Lord, I am the worst company in the world at a concert, I'm so apt to attend to the music.

Foppington: Why, Madam, that is very pardonable in the country, or at church; but a monstrous inattention in a polite assembly.[11]

D'Archenholz was severer: 'As the English in general, have no great attachment to this exotic entertainment, and are, for the most part, entirely ignorant of the language; this theatre is treated with the utmost contempt by the more sensible part of the people. The nobility alone support it: and they merely because—*it is the fashion*. There is not any place of entertainment in England where the audience *yawn* so much as there; its decorations, machinery, and wardrobe are altogether unworthy of the nation. There is nothing tolerable but its music. The great sums given by the managers to the *castratos*, who are better paid in England than any where, prevent them from laying out any money on the necessary decorations. The latter consequently enrich themselves, and the former have been constantly involved in difficulties.[12] To add to their offences, the Opera singers and dancers were 'all Italians, or French, and rank Papists.'[13]

A correspondent of the *London Chronicle* had a very different point of view to put forward. He argued that since audiences consisted 'of the first nobility, and persons of fortune, who have almost all of them been taught the Italian tongue, if not spent some part of their time in Italy, we shall be convinced, I believe,

11 *A Trip to Scarborough* (1777), II. i.
12 M. D'Archenholz, *A Picture of England* (Dublin, 1791), p. 234.
13 *London Chronicle*, 15–17 December 1757.

that the absurdity of sitting to hear what they do not understand is without foundation. The Opera properly belongs only to those; they are the encouragers, the supporters of the entertainment to which they come, as it were, *en famille*; and as any other persons that obtain admittance may in some sort be looked upon in the light of interlopers, they should, in my opinion, be extremely thankful for a pleasure which they could only receive by the interposition of their superiors.'[14]

Nothing could be more repugnant, however, to the honest Englishman than the castrati and their unnatural voices. A contributor of 'Plain Thoughts on Italian Operas' to the *Universal Magazine* declared, 'Of all the public sights I ever attended an opera . . . is the most despicable.' It was more than he could bear 'to sit two or three hours to see two or three emasculated objects of pity, with plaistered faces, whining with artificial voices.'[15] Another writer, probably puffing Covent Garden and Drury Lane, stated that both patent theatres were 'so well stored with excellent singers, that our fine connoisseurs will have an opportunity of feasting their ears without being obliged to gape at the nonsensical quality of a silly Eunuch, and of a whimsical Signora.'[16] Charles Churchill put the point more angrily:

> But never shall a Truly British age
> Bear a vile race of eunuchs on the stage.
> The boasted work's call'd National in vain,
> If one Italian voice pollutes the strain.[17]

The vanity of these bizarre foreigners was as insufferable as the impertinence of their claques. The latter were particularly objectionable and a newspaper correspondent denounced the managers for 'suffering the gallery, designed originally to accommodate persons of a certain rank, who through economy or accidental circumstances chose there to partake of the

14 11–14 November 1758. 15 lxv (1779), 35–6.
16 *The Gazetteer*, 26 September 1776.
17 *The Rosciad* (8th ed. 1763), lines 721–4.

amusement; I say, suffering the benches to be occupied by the very lowest class of people in this great city, namely that ignoble tribe attendant on the male and female singers. They are seated, if my information be good, *gratis*; their office to *puff* the Performers, in other words to impose by number and noise, and call aloud *applause* according to instruction—Nay, even in a Royal Presence, daring to call out *ancora* with a vociferation, noise of sticks and feet, in character only at the bear garden. . . . I can see no reason why this base crowd should not be placed among the footmen; and continue many of them, to wear a livery in the evening as well as in the morning.'[18]

Italian opera was disliked, then, because it was sung in a foreign language by some odd people with curious voices, and because it delighted a wealthy clique that claimed superior taste. Naturally this aroused a patriotic and Protestant opposition which wanted to see a native opera developed that would appeal to, and be understood by, a much larger section of society. Some attempts were made to satisfy this demand, but the only really successful one was Arne's *Artaxerxes. An English Opera* (1762). Even this had Italian antecedents, since Metastasio's *Artaserse* was translated to provide the libretto.

It was left to a German composer, trained in the Italian school but long resident in England, to satisfy the need for dramatic music sung in English. In 1741, Handel turned from Italian opera to concentrate on oratorio, a form that was similar to ancient Greek drama[19] in its lack of physical movement yet powerful expression of the feelings. By 1748 he had composed *Messiah, Samson, Joseph and his Brethren, Belshazzar,* the *Occasional Oratorio, Judas Maccabeus, Alexander Balus,* and *Joshua.* At the start, performances were well received, and Horace Walpole reported, on 24 February 1743, that Handel had 'set up an oratorio against the operas, and succeeds.'[20]

18 *London Chronicle*, 28–30 November 1765.
19 For resemblances to the Greek drama and to Racine, see P. H. Lang, *George Frideric Handel* (1967), pp. 367–83.
20 *Letters of Horace Walpole, ed. cit.*, i. 287.

Unfortunately the support was not maintained, even though Handel was resolutely English in his aims. On 17 January 1745, he wrote to the *Daily Advertiser* admitting that he could not go on: 'Having for a Series of Years received the greatest Obligations from the Nobility and Gentry of this Nation, I have always retained a deep Impression of their Goodness. As I perceived, that joining good Sense and significant Words to Musick, was the best Method of recommending *this* to an English Audience; I have directed my Studies that way, and endeavour'd to shew, that the English language, which is so expressive of the sublimest Sentiments is the best adapted of any to the full and solemn Kind of Musick. I have the Mortification now to find, that my Labours to please are become ineffectual. . . . '[21] The public felt compunction at this, and rallied behind him. He was able to give another ten of the twenty-four subscription concerts he had advertised, but then they came to an abrupt end with a third of the season still not completed. Handel fell ill from overwork, and was only brought back to creative life again by the advance of the Jacobite Charles Edward into England. The *Occasional Oratorio* was meant to stir Protestant hearts to combat; *Judas Maccabeus* was a celebration of the victory at Culloden, and *Joshua*, a paean in praise of conquest.

All three were performed at Covent Garden Theatre and it is interesting to find that this playhouse became the leading centre of Lenten oratorio performances, in its unbroken series between 1747 and 1773. They began under Handel's direction but were soon taken over by others, who rented the theatre for particular nights during Lent. Over the twenty-seven years, an average of nine performances a season were given, with *Judas Maccabeus*, *Messiah* and *Samson*, as the most popular of them.[22] Much less frequently rendered were *Jephtha*, *Deborah*, *Israel in Egypt*, and works that were not strictly oratorios, like

[21] Quoted by O. E. Deutsch, *Handel. A Documentary Biography* (1955), p. 602.

[22] *The London Stage* (ed. G. W. Stone), p. cxxxii.

L'Allegro and *Alexander's Feast*. Twenty pieces by Handel were represented in the repertory, a few by other composers were also included: Arne's *Judith*, Smith's *Rebecca*, Stanley's *Zimri*, and Arnold's *The Resurrection* and *Abimelech*.

Drury Lane's record was much less impressive. Between 1747 and 1769, oratorios were given there in only three seasons, and two of these (1750 and 1761) were very brief. From 1770 to 1773 and 1776 to 1778, the Drury Lane seasons were as active as those at Covent Garden. Occasional performances were also presented at the King's Theatre, and its most flourishing period lay in March 1768 and 1769. *Hannah*, with music by John Worgan and words by Christopher Smart, was sung there in 1764.

By tradition the playhouses closed during Passion Week, and, after they neglected to do so in 1752, the Lord Chamberlain ordered them 'not to act any Plays, Oratorios or any other Theatrical Performance in Passion Week for the Future on any Pretence whatsoever'.[23] This was observed until the end of the century and even into the nineteenth century, too. To herald the solemn period, Covent Garden devoted two nights before the closure to performances of *Messiah*. Not everyone approved of them because the libretto was made up of biblical quotations. One writer declared, 'An *Oratorio* either is an *Act* of *Religion*, or it is not; if it is, I ask if the *Playhouse* is a fit *Temple* to perform it in, or a Company of *Players* fit *Ministers* of *God's Word*.'[24] Yet the association of sublime music with the theatres and its performers added to their respectability, and it may be reasonably argued that the rise of oratorio in the Garrick period contributed as much to the standing of the theatres as it did to the musical life of the nation.

As far as the mass of the population was concerned the most delightful musical pieces were not to be found in the oratorio or Italian opera, but in the ballad operas and musical enter-

---

23 Quoted in O. E. Deutsch, *op. cit.*, p. 740, from P.R.O. L.C. 5/162, p. 2.
24 'Philalethes' in the *Universal Spectator*, 19 March 1743, quoted by O. E. Deutsch, p. 563.

tainments given at the patent theatres. Their airs were hummed and whistled throughout the Kingdom as well as in his Majesty's dominions overseas. Gay's *The Beggar's Opera* (1728) continued to be played frequently, but the record run of its first season was eventually challenged by Bickerstaffe's *Love in a Village*,[25] and passed by Sheridan's *The Duenna*. Even in the last quarter of the eighteenth century, these three were still among the chief attractions of the playhouses. When we count up the main pieces most frequently performed then, we find that *The School for Scandal* is first, and *Hamlet* fifth, in order. Between them come *The Beggar's Opera, Love in a Village*, and *The Duenna*.[26]

'Sing-song', as David Garrick called it, was immensely popular, and gave him a reason for leaving the country in 1763 for an extended stay on the continent. This idea was put forward in *A Dialogue in the Shades, between the celebrated Mrs. Cibber, and the no less celebrated Mrs. Woffington*:

Woffington: And is this all the entertainment the town has had for nine years?
Cibber: No, they have been mostly amused with comic operas, consisting of very indifferent poetry put to old tunes, without character, and scarcely any sentiment.
Woffington: Astonishing!
Cibber: And more so, when you consider that these harmonious pieces would fill houses, when Garrick and myself, in Shakespeare's best plays, could scarce pay expenses. This indeed, was the principal reason of the Manager's going abroad, and I think he would not have done wrong if he had never acted till the vicious taste of the town had been entirely corrected.[27]

Expectations of this sort were rather extravagant for the taste, vicious or otherwise, developed so greatly that Garrick felt its strength again in *The Duenna*; and the wits said of his last season that the old woman was too much for the old man.

---

25 See p. 113 below.
26 *The London Stage 1776–1800* (ed. C. B. Hogan, Carbondale, 1968), p. clxxi.
27 (1766), p. 14.

Many of these 'harmonious pieces' were rather trite, but a few reached high standards. Musically they appear to have carried on the Italian tradition, as Burney remarks: 'the English pasticcio burletta of *Love in a Village*, and . . . the *Maid of the Mill*, betrayed us into a taste for Italian melody, which has been the model of most of the vocal composers in and out of the theatre ever since. *The Duenna*, another favourite English pasticcio, in 1775, helped us on, and Dr. Arnold, Mr. Dibdin, and Mr. Shield, have very judiciously complied with the reigning taste, and imitated or adopted the opera style in all its vicissitudes.'[28] Yet he also admitted that Linley adhered to a style of his own in his elegies 'at least'. Another contemporary thought there was too much 'church music' in *The Duenna*.[29]

The best of these works ranged from rather slight musical entertainments, like *The Chaplet* by Moses Mendez and *Thomas and Sally* by Isaac Bickerstaff, to the carefully articulated plot of ballad (or comic) operas like *Love in a Village*, *Lionel and Clarissa*,[30] and *The Duenna*. Damon and Laura, Palaemon and Pastora, exchange love-plaints in verse in *The Chaplet*, and never descend to prose. The lyrics (set by Boyce) are pleasant enough, though lacking in distinction. In *Thomas and Sally* they are written in less stilted language, but Burney thought this piece succeeded only as a farce and that the music by Arne had little merit.

Love in a Village (1762) was altogether more ambitious. Bickerstaff admitted that it was based on Charles Johnson's *The Village Opera* (1729) and claimed nothing for it as dramatic writing, preferring to praise the music and to note that the airs were not common ballads. A table of over forty songs is appended to the printed edition: five were specially composed by Arne, two by Howard. Arne also drew on tunes he had earlier composed. Others were by Weldon, Baildon, Festing,

---

28 C. Burney, *op. cit.*, ii. 1016.
29 James Barry: see A. Lefanu, *Memoirs of the Life and Writings of Mrs. Frances Sheridan* (1824), pp. 403–4.
30 See p. 116 below.

Giardini, Handel, Galuppi, Geminiani, Paradies, and Boyce. The best-known of them was 'My heart's my own, my will is free', which became the anthem of all undutiful daughters. Another expresses the yearning of Justice Woodcock for earlier days and joys:

> When I follow'd a lass that was froward and shy,
> Oh! I stuck to her stuff, till I made her comply;
> Oh! I took her so lovingly round the waist,
> And I smack'd her lips and held her fast:
>   When hug'd and haul'd,
>   she squeal'd and squall'd;
> But though she vow'd all I did was in vain,
> Yet I pleased her so well, that she bore it again:
>   Then hoity, toity,
>   Whisking, frisking,
> Green was her gown upon the grass;
> Oh! such were the joys of our dancing days.[31]

As is usual in Bickerstaff's pieces, downright and opinionated characters are revealed with gusto. In fact, the great popularity of *Love in a Village* was derived not only from its pleasing music but from its spirited dialogue and characterisation.

The success of a similar piece, *The Maid of the Mill*, led to Bickerstaff's being offered a contract to produce further work for Covent Garden Theatre, and its terms are interesting because they give us an idea of contemporary practice in these matters and the author's own standing. He agreed that he would deliver the managers[32] before the first of September 1766

compleat Copy of a New Comic opera or Dramatic performance written by him & called Love in the City or by whatsoever Title together with the Score of the Music properly adapted thereto and therewith to be performed at the said Theatre & also before 1 September 1768 another Comic opera and score of the Music &c. &c

31 Act II, Sc. 3.
32 Between 1761 and 1767, they were Priscilla Rich (John Rich's widow) and the tenor, John Beard.

and that the said Isaac Bickerstaff shall & will attend all Rehearsals
or practice of said operas and assist in properly preparing the same
for the first publick representation on the Stage of the said Theatre.
Said I. Bickerstaff shall not within said 5 Year from 1 September
next Introduce produce or deliver directly or undirectly any play
opera or other Dramatic piece or performance or any part thereof
he is or shall be composer or Compiler of to any person concerned in
the direction or Management of any other Theatre or cause any of
them to be publicly exhibited or represented at any other Theatre
except as thereafter mentioned without Licence or writing first
obtained. When said Dramatic pieces are accepted they shall be
prepared for representation & the 3 – 6 – 9 Nights of publick
representation of such of them as shall have a run or continue to be
performed for Nine Nights—pay or cause to be paid to said I.
Bickerstaff whatever shall be remaining of the Money which shall
be received on the said 3d – 6th & 9th Nights after the usual
charges[33] are deducted. Should the Managers reject or decline
performance of any Comic opera by said I. Bickerstaff it shall be
lawfull for him to get the same represented at any other Theatre in
great Britain or Ireland—when any of the said operas have been
represented Nine Nights it shall be lawfull for said Isaac Bickerstaff
to get them acted in any Theatre in the Kingdom of Ireland only.[34]

The contract was important because Garrick soon saw that
Bickerstaff was a very useful acquisition at Covent Garden
and wondered if he could bring him into his own service. What
happened then is described in the *Universal Museum*: 'That
gentleman was pleased with the prospect of a connection with
Garrick, and therefore indulged him with a little piece he had
prepared for this season, called *Incle and Yarico*. The musick
was frequently played over at Hampton, and the latter part of
the summer was passed in *billing* and *cooing* between these two
geniuses. In short, matters were settled as far as lay in Mr.
B——ff's power. He wished it, but was unfortunately under
articles to Mr. Beard, &c. for a certain term of years, to supply

[33] £64. 5s. od.
[34] Folger MS. T. a. 66, ff. 1–3: James Winston's notes from Arthur
Murphy's papers. I have expanded the abbreviations.

so many pieces every season. However, he thought, as the management of the house had got into other hands, he might be free; but, alas! he had *pawned his brains*, if I may so call it, with Mr. Beard, for something under a hundred pounds.'[35] The new managers refused to release him, and 'the little piece' was not performed.

His contract was dated 4 May 1765, and the penalty for infringement was one thousand pounds. He now fulfilled his obligations by writing *Love in the City* (1767), *Lionel and Clarrisa* (1768),[36] and *The Padlock* (1768). All were well received, for they had a liveliness that audiences loved, and lightly drawn characters that were eagerly taken by players. His plain-spoken young women and old men were very popular. Priscilla Tomboy was a most famous hoyden and was given new life later in the century by Mrs. Jordan. Jenny, the maidservant in *Lionel and Clarissa*, complains that her master 'wanted to be rude with her,' and voices her disapproval strongly in the song, 'A servant, I hope, is no slave.' Her openness and racy language are to be seen in her counsel to her young mistress to stop weeping for her 'eyes are as red as a ferret's.' Colonel Oldboy is a sensual blusterer, but he is cunning enough to divert his wife's grievances by pretending to find a spider on her petticoat. Don Diego (in *The Padlock*) licks his negro servant, Mungo, every day with a rattan, and wants to marry an innocent girl of sixteen, but is quickly persuaded by Leander that the difference in their ages makes them incompatible. Bickerstaff is careful to show the different points of view of his characters and they influence each other to an extent that is rather surprising in the over-conventional world of eighteenth-century drama. For example, Sir John is indignant, in *Lionel and Clarissa*, because the young people have behaved hypocritically towards him by pretending to obey his wishes, then running away. Jenkins puts their behaviour to him in another light: 'Call it by a gentler name, Sir, modesty on her part, apprehension on his.' A

---

35 III (1767), 557–8.
36 Revised in 1770 as *The School for Fathers*.

cool good-humour counters the violent outbursts of some of the characters, and gives perspective and naturalism to libretti, which are so likeable that several of them have been revived in our own day.

The first page of Sheridan's manuscript *The Duenna*.

Bickerstaff's success was only surpassed in his period by R. B. Sheridan. The dialogue of *The Duenna* (1775) is fluent and sufficiently pointed for its purpose, and the characterisation is always adequate. In the case of Isaac Mendoza, 'the dupe of his own art', it is brilliantly sketched. The plot is cleverly handled, even though it is rather stagey. The lyrics have a charm of their own, and were remarkably popular. The superintendent of the music was Thomas Linley, who contributed some pieces himself and levied others from his son Tom, as well as from William Jackson of Exeter, Galliard, Michael Arne, Giordani, Hayes and others. The words vary in mood from the comic 'Give Isaac the nymph who no beauty can boast', through the ruefulness of 'If a daughter you have, she's the plague of your life', to the pathos of 'Soft pity never leaves the gentle breast.' The enduring quality of the work can be seen in the successive arrangements of the music by a number of composers, and the fairly recent adaptations of the libretto by Roberto Gerhard and for Serge Prokofiev.

Sheridan's *The Camp* (1778) was almost as successful in its first year of production, but its subject was topical and did not maintain interest. It lacks the sparkle of *The Duenna*, for its appeal lay in rough humour, rousing military airs, and De Loutherbourg's scenery.[37]

When we turn from opera in its various forms and oratorio to consider the place of ballet or dancing in this period, we find less of a contrast between the kinds of entertainment at the King's Theatre and those given in the patent theatres.

Burney thought dancing did little to attract the public to the King's Theatre in 1743, and that it did not 'gain the ascendant over Music' until 1772–3, when Anne Heinel appeared there.[38] He does not mention, however, the brilliance of Giovanni Gallini between the scenes of *Attalo* in 1758, when the *London Chronicle* reported, 'he not only gives the strongest proof of his executive powers, but also of his skill in designing, by having composed three of the prettiest ballets I ever saw; and for plot, movement, humour, and, if I may make use of the expression,

---

[37] See p. 82.
[38] C. Burney, *op. cit.*, ii. 842, 878.

gesticulated wit, they are equal, I believe, to any of those which Lewis the Fourteenth was so fond of.'

The ballet that accompanied opera did not always satisfy the fastidious. Algarotti thought the dances were monotonous and 'nothing better than an unnatural caprioling . . . an illiberal skipping about, which ought never to be applauded by persons of a polite education, being as it were a perpetual monotony of a very few steps, and of as few figures.'³⁹ His classical principles were outraged by the irrational contrast that they presented: 'As soon as an act is over, several dancers sally forth on the stage, who have no manner of affinity with the plan of the piece. For, if the scene of the action be Rome, the dance is often made to be in Cusco, or in Pekin; and if the Opera be serious, the dance is sure to be comic.'⁴⁰ English audiences at the patent theatres would have found this more acceptable for, by tradition, contrast provided relief, and *King Lear* could be properly followed by a dance called 'the Frolick'.

In fact, the patent theatres saw a much wider variety of dances than the King's Theatre. At the highest level, we find the great ballet-master, J.-G. Noverre, bringing his company to Drury Lane in 1755 to present *The Chinese Festival*.⁴¹ His ideas about ballet were to be expressed in his *Lettres sur la Danse, et sur les Ballets*,⁴² with an advocacy of diversification in place of the mechanical rigidity of balanced groups. Ballet should reveal a living picture of the passions, manners and ceremonies of the peoples of the earth, and through the use of pantomime speak to the soul through the eyes. This was what was achieved in *The Chinese Festival*, as presented in London: 'the scenery was superb and the dresses magnificent. The procession was composed of ninety persons; the palanquin and the chariots were very rich. . . . The round-dance, in which there were forty-eight performers, was executed with a precision and neatness such as are not ordinary in grand ballets; in a word, those *Fêtes chinoises*, which achieved so brilliant a success at Paris,

³⁹ *An Essay on the Opera* (1768), p. 66.   ⁴⁰ *Ibid.*, p. 65.
⁴¹ Cf. p. 97.   ⁴² (Lyon, 1760), pp. 10–18.   119

were nothing in comparison with these in London. The
expenses amounted to two thousand louis.'[43]

Dances at the patent theatres were normally much less
elaborate. Some of them simply represented well-known figures
like the minuet. Others were national in origin, like the
'Savoyards' at Drury Lane on 20 March 1749 or the 'grand
Dutch dance' at Covent Garden on 19 March 1752.[44] Many
described the ritual of work by harvesters, faggot binders, or
coopers.[45] To this kind belonged 'The Threshers', danced at
Covent Garden in 1758. It was drawn from an old Italian
ballet: 'Mr. Lucas and Mr. Leppie shew a great deal of
laughable drollery, and Mademoiselle Capdeville is by a
thousand degrees the best woman dancer on the English stage.[46]
In the same week, Grimaldi[47] had made his début at Drury
Lane in *The Millers*, and a newspaper commented: 'Some
people hold dancing to be below the dignity of a regular
Theatre; but I can by no means subscribe to their opinion;
since one of the principal ends of every theatre is to delight. . . .
I shall not affect to shew my learning, by adding that the
Ancients not only admitted Dancing, but thought it a necessary
Ornament in the performance of the most celebrated tragedies.
The French for many years carried all before them in this kind
of merit; but of late the Italians seem to have got the start of
them; and it must be allowed that the latter are much better
actors, which in the comic dance which now prevails almost
every where, is infinitely more requisite, than those graceful
postures and movements on which the French dancers, for the
most part, pique themselves. . . . Grimaldi is a man of great
strength and agility; he indeed treads the air. If he has any
fault, he is rather too comical; and from some feats which I

43 F. A. Hedgcock, . . . *David Garrick and his French Friends* (1911), p.
131, quoting the *Journal Étranger*, Dec. 1755, p. 233.
44 *The London Stage* (ed. G. W. Stone), pp. 105, 301.
45 *Ibid.*, pp. 1037, 1043, 1101.
46 *London Chronicle*, 14–17 October 1758.
47 Giuseppe Grimaldi, pantomimist and father of the celebrated clown,
'Joe'.

have been witness to his performing, at the King's Theatre in the Haymarket, it is my opinion that those spectators will see him with most pleasure, who are least solicitous whether he breaks his neck or not.'[48]

For the most thoughtful of comments on these dances, we have to turn to William Hogarth's *Analysis of Beauty*, for the great artist had attentively considered the aesthetics of ballet at this period: 'Dances that represent provincial characters . . . or very low people, such as gardeners, sailors, etc. in merriment, are generally most entertaining on the stage: the Italians have lately added great pleasantry and humour to several French dances, particularly the wooden-shoe dance, in which there is a continual shifting from one attitude in plain lines to another; both the man and woman often comically fix themselves in uniform positions, and frequently start in equal time, with angular forms, one of which remarkably represents two W's in a line . . .; these sort of dances a little raised, especially on the woman's side, in expressing elegant wantonness (which is the true spirit of dancing) have of late years been most delightfully done, and seem at present to have got the better of pompous, unmeaning grands ballets; serious dancing being even a contradiction in terms.'[49]

Many of the dancers were themselves French or Italian, so when Signor and Signora Zuchelli took part in 'the mummery of the new ballet at Covent Garden called "The Gardeners",' the *Morning Chronicle* thought that it might be wise to banish 'every foreign Mâitre de danse from Drury Lane and Covent Garden to the [King's] Theatre in the Haymarket, where foppery and folly triumph over reason.'[50] But Acres represented many an Englishman in having 'anti-Gallican toes'. Even more of them disliked serious ballet and serious opera as the pastimes of finicking foreigners and their wrong-headed admirers.

48 *London Chronicle*, 14–17 October 1758.
49 *Works of Hogarth* (ed. T. Clerk, 1810), ii. 150.
50 6 November 1775.

I

Performers of opera, oratorio, and ballet enhanced the claim of the patent houses to be considered as centres of the arts in the mid-eighteenth-century London. If comic opera and comic dances were preferred to the more serious types, that was the trend of the age and faithfully represented the taste of the majority of spectators. The castrati, like some of the French ballet dancers, found a home in a subscription theatre and were content to give delight to a wealthy minority.

Barry as Othello.

CHAPTER SEVEN

Topical Criticism

Criticism of any new play began in the most practical way possible at the end of the first performance. The prompter came on and announced a second representation. If this was vigorously applauded, the play was given again; if hisses were more frequent, the play was damned.

So much depended on the first night's verdict that it is hardly surprising to learn that claques were employed to sway opinion. The German clergyman, G. W. Alberti, who visited England between 1745 and 1747, warned foreigners not to take demonstrations on behalf of a play too seriously since the theatres themselves packed the house with claqueurs. He also mentioned that agreement to damn a play was sometimes made before performance[1] and this is supported by the writer of *A Letter to Mr. G——k Relative to his Treble Capacity of Manager, Actor, and Author* (1749):

A Gentleman that sat next to me, soon as the Play was over, said to his Friend, *Now for it, have you got your Cat-call? Yes, yes,* reply'd the other, *I never go without my Tackle,* and immediately try'd the Force of his Instrument. Others were prepar'd as strenuously to support it; so that I don't think there were three People, besides myself, that intended Justice. This the Consequence prov'd; for both Sides were so ready to approve and condemn, that I could not hear distinctly one Sentence.[2]

[1] J. A. Kelly, *German Visitors to English Theaters*, p. 23.   [2] P. 16.   123

A curious example of the extremes to which opposing sides could go was shown in March 1770, when Hugh Kelly's *A Word to the Wise* was acted at Drury Lane Theatre. The comedy itself was the last thing the audience wanted to consider. Kelly had written political articles for the administration, and was therefore still assumed to be a government hireling. Hissing began at once, then calls for Garrick and the damning of the play. When the prompter followed custom by asking whether it should be given again on the next night of performance, the supporters of Kelly equalled in number the antiministerial faction, so no decision was reached. *A Word to the Wise* was advertised, however, for representation two nights later, but uproar prevented it from being given. Garrick tried to soothe the opposition by making a personal appeal to the audience, but he could hardly be heard, and his pleas were ignored. The audience disbanded after several hours of noisy disagreement, and its money was returned. The play was withdrawn and had to wait until May 1777 before it could be judged, in the theatre, on its own merits.

'Parties' were not confined to political subjects, but might be formed for the sake of aesthetic principles, too. Goldsmith noted in 1759, that 'as our pleasures, as well as more important concerns, are generally managed by party, the stage is subject to its influence. The managers, and all who espouse their side, are for decoration and ornament; the critic, and all who have studied French decorum, are for regularity and declamation.'[3] And a similar attitude was expressed in 1766 by the author of *A Dialogue in the Shades:* 'Everything upon the stage, as well as in many other places, is entirely conducted by party, and if an author is so lucky as to ingratiate himself with the leading theatrical critics, he may bring on whatever trash he pleases, and be sure of success.'[4]

The 'critics in the pit' were undoubtedly influential, but there is evidence to suggest that their dominance began to wane as the newspapers and magazines grew in critical

124   [3] *Collected Works* (ed. Friedman), I. 323.   [4] P. 16.

authority. Tate Wilkinson made this clear when he declared, 'The pit critics . . . decided all disputes, damnations, etc., which at present, to save the audience trouble, the morning papers have taken most of the grand articles of setting up or knocking down.'[5]

Between 1741 and 1756, there were few notices in periodicals that would be considered theatrical critiques as the term is now understood. In its four years of existence *The World* printed only four general essays on stage topics; six appeared in *The Connoisseur*. Samuel Johnson showed no interest in the subject in *The Rambler* and *The Idler*,[6] but his characteristic style has been traced in five notices of plays in the *Gentleman's Magazine*.[7] For the most part, they used the formula that was common at the time: a lengthy summary of the plot was followed by critical comment that might be full but was usually brief. On Moore's *Gil Blas*, judgement was damning: it had 'not one elegant expression, or moral sentiment in the dialogue; nor indeed character in the drama.'[8] The reviewer was kinder to the same playwright's *The Gamester*, saying it was 'heighten'd with many tender incidents, and, as the dialect is perfectly colloquial, it probably produced a greater effect upon the majority of the audience than if it had been decorated with beauties.'[9] The word 'probably' reveals, I think, that the critic had read the play but had not seen it in the theatre.

Arthur Murphy's essays in the *Gray's Inn Journal* (1752–4),[10] John Hill's as 'The Inspector' in *The London Daily Advertiser* (1751–2), and those by Paul Hiffernan in *The Tuner* (1754–5), contained many more theatrical allusions; and Hill and Hiffernan lost no opportunity of discussing stage practice. For example, Hiffernan reviewed Hogarth's *Analysis of Beauty* and

5 *Memoirs*, iv. 82.
6 See C. H. Gray, *Theatrical Criticism in London to 1795* (New York, 1931; repr. 1964), pp. 97–104.
7 D. J. Greene, 'Was Johnson Theatrical Critic of the *Gentleman's Magazine?*' *R.E.S.*, N.S., iii (1952), 158–61.
8 xxi (1751), 77–8.   9 xxiii (1753), 61.
10 For comment, see C. H. Gray, *op. cit.*, pp. 120–4

said, 'let me observe to You the Affinity of his Doctrine to the Rules of the Stage. In every perfect *Drama* the *Line of Beauty* must prevail. . . . His Principles will appear illustrated in every perfect Production for the Theatres—to wit—FITNESS, VARIETY, UNIFORMITY, SIMPLICITY, INTRICACY, QUANTITY.'[11] It is unlikely that anyone ever sees a perfect drama or perfect production, and the phrasing is rather typical of Hiffernan's over-enthusiastic approach. 'Railing and praising were his usual themes.' and as a sample of his disgust we may cite the opening of his notice of *Philoclea*: the play was 'an Outlaw from all the Rules of Criticism; the Unities of Time, Place, and Action are all unobserved; Plot, Moral, Verisimilitude, or even Probability unknown; many Scenes bid Defiance to Possibility.'[12]

His criteria were the conventional ones of the day, and it took a more acute critic to see that even Shakespeare came off badly, judged by some of these requirements. A stronger emphasis must therefore be placed on truth to character, and this is what we find in a series of notices which appeared in the *London Chronicle* in 1757. A recent writer has stated that it deserves 'to rank with the work of the later critics, like Leigh Hunt and William Hazlitt, as vivid and intelligent writing about the contemporary stage', and has tentatively ascribed it to Arthur Murphy, because of Johnson's guess that Murphy was the author of the encomium of his proposals for an edition of Shakespeare, that appeared in the issue of 12–14 April 1757.[13] All that otherwise can be discovered about the writer is that he signed himself 'Tragicomicus' when he proposed the series.

His suggestions were novel in their insistence on a shorter summary of the plot and, by implication, on a long and thorough criticism, by new standards, of the acting and the theatrical qualities of the play: 'I could wish to see a short Analysis of every Play, with a summary Account of its Merit or Deficiency, and whether it owes its Reception to Character, Wit, Humour, and Incident combined, or to any one of those Requisites . . . accompanied with Criticisms on the acting,

11 P. 28.   12 P. 41.   13 C. H. Gray, *op. cit.*, pp. 106–33.

not calculated to give Pain to the Performer, but derived from the Source of Nature, Taste and Good Sense.'[14]

He took as his opening subject Aaron Hill's adaptation of Voltaire's *Meropé*, first performed in London in 1749 and revived on 22 January 1757. Voltaire thought it the masterpiece among his fugitive writings, and the critic was ready to agree that the distress of the Queen in the third act when about to sacrifice her son, formed one of the most pathetic scenes to be found on any stage. After this, interest weakened: 'the Play never rises to anything like a Climax of Terror and Pity . . . which is in general too much neglected by the French Writers.' Hill had done nothing to improve it, but had rendered it 'strongly sentimental'.[15]

Hill's adaptation of Voltaire's *Zaïre* (as *Zara*) also met with an unfavourable reception: 'The Character of Osman has a dignified Elevation of Mind; but the Distress is hardly anywhere brought to that Degree of acute Feeling which we find in the Tragedies of Shakespeare and Otway. Lusignan is very well sketched, and receives infinitely more beautiful Touches from the exquisite Pencil of Mr. Garrick, than it owes to the Hand of the Poet.'[16]

The *London Chronicle* writer was prepared to admit that Voltaire was a sound critic sometimes, and noted in a review of *Cato* that the Frenchman had 'justly observed that the Love Plot throws a Languor over the Whole: The Business, during the Scenes of softer Passion, always stand still; and is therefore uninteresting.' Even so, the Englishman argued, *Cato* was a work of genius in its nobility of scenes and sentiment, polished language, and developed central character. It had 'Flights of Elevation beyond the Modern Muse's Wing.'[17]

On Shakespearean performances the remarks of this *London Chronicle* critic were equally discriminating. *Macbeth* showed 'amazing proof of our Author's Insight into Nature, who has,

14 *London Chronicle*, 18–20 January 1757.
15 *Ibid.*, 22–25 January 1757.
16 *Ibid.*, 27–29 January 1757.   17 *Ibid.*, 5–8 February 1757.

in three different Characters, separated the Workings of
Remorse, and shewn its Operation to be productive of remarkable Effects in each, according to their respective Tempers.'
Its style was peculiar, 'abounding in Words infrequent in their
use, but remarkably strong and picturesque.' On the subject
of the witches—'a machinery so whimsical'—he recommended
his readers to see Mr. Johnson's small pamphlet, *Miscellaneous
Observations on the Tragedy of Macbeth.*[18] *Measure for Measure*
contained a fine variety of passions, but Shakespeare had 'un-
necessarily overcharged it with supernumerary Incidents, which
do not conduce to the main Business, and he has crouded it
with episodical Characters.'[19] One of the greatest attractions
of *Much Ado about Nothing* was Garrick's speech when he 'first
deliberates whether he shall marry Beatrice. His Manner of
coming forth from the Arbour, and the Tone of his Voice, when
he says, "This is no Trick," etc., is diverting in the highest
Degree.' [20] Yet in *Henry IV, Part I*, 'the Players have agreed to
supersede one of the best Scenes in the Play, which is that
between Falstaff and the Prince, where Sir John personates by
turns the King and his Son, with such a Vein of Humour as
perhaps would divert an Audience beyond anything in the
Comedy.'[21]

When he examined the work of other playwrights, his mind
was alert in seeking the beauties and the deformities of every
production. He declared that 'the Circumstance on which the
Catastrophe [of Otway's *The Orphan*] turns is rather gross and
shocking.'[22] In Fielding's plays, 'there is sometimes Irregularity,
Hurry and Inadvertence, yet there is always infinite Pleasantry,
and, in Shakespeare's words, "He never wants the natural
Touch." '[23] *The Alchymist* was interesting chiefly because
Garrick played Drugger, but its humour in general was
'frequently unintelligible'.[24] Mrs. Behn's *The Rover* and

18 *London Chronicle*, 24 February–1 March 1757.
19 *Ibid.*, 3–5 March 1757.   20 *Ibid.*, 19–22 March 1757.
21 *Ibid.*, 25 January 1757.   22 *Ibid.*, 8–10 March 1757.
23 *Ibid.*, 10–12 February 1757.   24 *Ibid.*, 5–8 March 1757.

Shadwell's *Fair Quaker of Deal*[25] were beneath criticism, but *The Rover* required strong censure because of its lowness:

One of the Personages of the Drama takes off his Breeches in the Sight of the Audience, whose Diversion is of a complicated Nature on this Occasion. The Ladies are first alarmed; then the Men stare: The Women put up their Fans—'My Lady Betty, what is the Man about?—Lady Mary, sure he is "not in earnest!" ' Then peep thro' their Fans—'Well, I vow, the He-creature is taking off his odious Breeches—He—he—Po!—is that all?—the Man has Drawers on.' ... Meantime, the Delight of the Male Part of the Audience is occasioned by the various Operations of this Phaenomenon on the Female Mind—'This is rare Fun, d--n me—Jack, Tom, Bob, did you ever see anything like this?—Look at that Lady yonder—See, in the Stage Box—how she looks half averted,' etc., etc. It is a Matter of Wonder that the Upper Gallery don't call for a Hornpipe, or, 'Down with the Drawers,' according to their Custom of insisting upon as much as they can get for their Money. But to be a little serious, it should be remembered by all Managers that this Play was written in the dissolute Days of Charles the Second; and that Decency at least is, or ought to be, demanded at present.[26]

This kind of impropriety needed condemnation in comedy, and another sort required it in tragedy. His example, Congreve's *The Mourning Bride*, was taken from the same Restoration period and was shown to be as severely wanting in taste as some tragedies of the mid-fifties: 'Audiences when *The Mourning Bride* was wrote, were chiefly fond of being elevated and surprised, and indeed the same vicious Relish seems to recommence at present; other wise we should not see Plays received with Applause, when their chief merit consists in Trick, Incident, and Business, without character, Fable, or Language. *The Mourning Bride* is not entirely defective in the three last-mentioned Particulars: *Zara* is a commanding character; the Vicissitudes of her Rage and Love; her noble Propensities, and the Vehemence of her Passions, which *tear her Virtues up*, are all

---

25 *Ibid.*, 22–24 February, 10–12 March 1757.
26 *Ibid.*, 22–24 February 1757.

drawn in very fine Proportions. *Osmyn* is likewise a character well conceived: The first Introduction of him is very striking, and his Exit at the Close of the first Act, leaves the Mind in a pause of Suspense . . . the recognizing Scene between him and Almeria [shows] Joy and Tenderness, affectingly mingled. After this, the Remainder of Osmyn's Part is all Rant and wild Poetry, the Ideas and Expressions being drawn from the Stores of the Imagination, without the Simplicity always natural to Emotions of the Heart. The rest of the Piece is a Succession of Miracles, unnatural and improbable Turns of Fortune; and we are every Moment surprized with some new Discovery to make us stare, but not to reach our Hearts. However, upon the Whole, this Tragedy is on the side of Virtue, and in that Respect, and that only, it is the best of all Mr. Congreve's Plays.'[27]

The critic feared that audiences were too easily satisfied with situation and stage business, and reverted to this subject in several of his critiques. Of Beaumont and Fletcher's *The Chances* (revised by Buckingham), he said: 'The Play owes its Success principally to quick Turns of Business, a Variety of Incidents, and some diverting Situations.'[28] In Vanbrugh's *The Provoked Wife*, the dialogue was natural and the fable well conducted, 'full of what the Players call Business, tending to produce entertaining Situations, and frequent Opportunities for lively Traits of Character.'[29] Mrs. Centlivre's dialogue was 'very paltry in general, and the Characters are not marked with any separating Peculiarities unless the Jealousy of Don Felix be accounted such. As Mrs. Centlivre understood the stage, she has contrived to keep the Attention of her Audience alive by a very quick succession of scenes. . . . This Play [*The Wonder*] is a Proof that what the Players call Business will succeed without Writing, when it is in the Hands of such excellent Performers.'[30]

Much could be conveyed in the theatre without the use of words: gesture, movement, miming, all carried meaning, and

27 *London Chronicle*, 25–27 January 1757.
28 *Ibid.*, 25–27 January 1757.
29 *Ibid.*, 1–3 March 1757.   30 *London Chronicle*, 1–3 February 1775.

stagey plays were mere sets of directions improved on by the actors. But fine plays and performances were very different. When Garrick and Mrs. Cibber starred in *The Orphan*, they were said 'to warm and animate each other', and great actors in general had much the same relationship with great plays. The only place to appreciate this was the playhouse itself, but the drama had been discussed too often in the past by those who read printed copies and were eager to formulate theories that echoed the ideas of critics ancient and modern. The time had come to weigh the total effect of a play in its natural home. To arrive at understanding and at truth, one question must be asked: did the play reveal 'Nature, Taste, and Good Sense'?

The *London Chronicle* critic did not demand conformity to any other rules, though he clearly expected that the tone of plays should conform to the decent standards of society. He seemed to suggest, too, that 'writing' would succeed only when dialogue was true to character, and characterisation was true to itself. Tragedy should elevate the mind, touch the heart, and quicken the spirits. Comedy should reconcile us to life. All this was implicit (and was sometimes stated) in his critiques, and they form a lively guide to the changes in outlook of the period.

The *London Chronicle* printed another series of articles on the theatre in 1758, and some of them show the same attitudes as were to be found in 1757. For example, plays by Farquhar and Mrs. Centlivre were treated with severity. 'No picture was less taken from the life' than Serjeant Kite in *The Recruiting Officer*, and Plume and Balance were 'the only figures in the whole piece which carry any marks of that imitation which constitutes the excellence of dramatic painting.'[31] The plot of Mrs. Centlivre's *The Wonder* was 'in some respects exquisitely beautiful', but 'when you have said this, you have said everything, for the Language is contemptible to the last degree.'[32] Pantomime was discussed in the old way: of *Queen Mab*, the critic wrote, 'I have not yet seen this farce above seven and thirty times; but as soon as I am able to find out the design of it, I shall communi-

31 *London Chronicle*, 5–7 October 1758.   32 *Ibid.*, 7–10 October 1758.   131

cate my thoughts upon that subject.' It is possible that more than one writer contributed these articles, for the range is wider than it had been in the previous year, and took in opera[33] and 'pantomime dance'.[34] Whoever the critic was he possessed good judgement and a thorough knowledge of theatrical effect in all its branches. Mrs. Clive's Lady Wishfor't 'is indeed a ridiculous character, but she shews a ridiculous woman of quality; whereas all the actresses that have hitherto performed the part have dressed themselves like mad women, and acted in the strain of an old nurse. A high fruze[35] tower, a gaudy petticoat of one sort, and a gown of another, was sure to create a laugh; but Mrs. Clive is not obliged to have recourse to any such pityful expedients. Accordingly she dresses the part in the pink of the present mode and makes more of it than any actress ever did.'[36] The parting scene between Lord and Lady Townly was criticised for the meanness of the catastrophe: 'For Lady Townly's reformation is effected by the most abject and mercenary of all principles, the fear of future want, and the hope of returning fortune.'[37] He was glad to know that Southerne's stock play, *The Fatal Marriage*, had been shortened, gave a reasoned case to support his opinion of it, and ended by showing that authority was on his side:

The Tragi-comedy now before us is made up of an amazing Succession of Scenes wholly detached from each other, and like an April Day, it is one moment overcast with melancholy Gloom and instantly brightens into Chearfulness and Pleasure. For instance, the Play opens with a Scene between Fabian, Frederick, and Jacqueline; after which, the two last ingeniously contrive to fasten a Letter to Fernando's coat behind, that he may be the unconscious Carrier of it to his Daughter; then Villeroy and Carlos enter, and talk of business very different from the foregoing; then another Scene in Fernando's House, when the Letter is pleasantly taken from the old Man's coat; to this succeeds Isabella, with her little Son; after her Distress is painted forth, we have more comic Scenes between

---

33 See pp. 107–8.   34 See pp. 120–1.   35 Frizzy tower of hair.
36 *London Chronicle*, 14–16 November 1758.
37 *Ibid.*, 9–11 March 1758, reviewing *The Provok'd Husband*.

Fàbian Ja[c]queline, etc. . . . next, pleasant Intrigue, dark Lanthorns and Ladders of Ropes; now a supposed Widow in her Weeds, then a Young Girl in Breeches; this moment an afflicted Mother weeping over her Orphan, and a Minute after, an old Man buried alive, bursting out of his Tomb, and then we are diverted with the comical Humours of his thinking himself dead, and smelling himself. Mr. Dryden,[38] who, in compliance with the false Taste of his Cotemporaries, fell into this vicious Practice himself, has, notwithstanding, expressed himself with great good Sense in regard to this heterogeneous Mixture of Passions altogether destructive of one another.[39]

'Good sense' was effectively contrasted with 'false Taste' in this example and many other theatrical notices that appeared in the *London Chronicle* in 1757 and 1758.[40]

They were not typical of reviews of plays in the newspapers and magazines of the next twenty years, for prejudice and 'party' were sometimes evident and merely pedestrian reporting even more frequent.

In the sixties some nine newspapers and thirteen magazines printed snippets of theatre gossip, very brief comments on the printed drama, summaries of the plots of plays, short excerpts of dialogue, or, much more occasionally, full notices. As far as we can tell from files that are sometimes incomplete, not one of them produced serious critical articles on the theatre regularly over a long period.

Hugh Kelly's *The Babler* (1767) was advertised as containing 'a careful selection from those Entertaining and Interesting Essays which have given the Public so much Satisfaction under that Title during a Course of Four Years in Owens's Weekly Chronicle,' but the articles in the two volumes were not confined to theatrical subjects and were not reviews of particular plays. They were most interesting when they criticised the

---

38 'An Essay of Dramatic Poesy' in *Essays of John Dryden* (ed. W. P. Ker, Oxford, 1900), i. 57–8.
39 *London Chronicle*, 6–8 December 1757.
40 For a fuller account and different examples, see C. H. Gray, *op. cit.*, pp. 128–45.

critics. Kelly noted that many writers now noted a 'visible decay in Dramatic productions' as compared with those of the past half-century. He replied, 'The gentlemen who criticise in this accurate manner, seem, however, to pay but little attention to the original institution of the stage: they imagine it was entirely calculated for amusement, without having the least view to the great business of instruction, and so it could produce a ridiculous laugh, no matter what became either of our morals or our understandings.' This led him to say that he admired Wycherley, Congreve, and Vanbrugh as men of wit, 'yet as dramatic authors, I hold them in no extraordinary estimation.' They were guilty of 'a culpable degree of levity' and 'the rankest indecencies.' He concluded that 'the writers of our present times, however despised by the bigots of a dramatical heresy, have . . . an infinitely stronger claim to our admiration than any of their celebrated predecessors.'[41] This will seem grossly exaggerated if we do not emphasise that he was thinking of their predecessors from the Restoration period onwards. Wit was for him 'but a secondary requisite to a dramatic poet; judgement is the first qualification.' And judgement, to Kelly and others of his day, was based on a proper sensibility, a knowledge of the human heart.

Another magazine, *The Monitor* (1767), was willing to admit that some of the characters in Goldsmith's *The Good-Natur'd Man* were drawn with 'a very masterly hand', but thought that the play itself was greatly inferior in sentiments to Kelly's *False Delicacy*. This judgement was taken up by 'A Despiser of Imposition', who claimed that many of Kelly's sentiments were proverbial and went on to make a strong distinction between such commonplaces and the sentiments that arose 'from superior knowledge and the most delicate feelings.'[42] In a different issue, a reviewer deplored the fact that Steele's and Addison's plays were so seldom performed. They 'strictly adhered to decency and morality', while Restoration plays, so often presented,

41 Pp. 23–6. *The Babler* is not mentioned by C. H. Gray.
42 6 and 27 February 1768.

were thoroughly immoral. Congreve's Sharper had made many pickpockets, and the example of Valentine, many spendthrifts. 'The habit of attending to . . . vice, has such an effect by being rendered familiar in jest, that the power of resisting it is lost, even with those who wish to oppose it.'[43]

A third periodical, the *Universal Museum*, paid steady attention to the theatre from the magazine's foundation in 1762 to the end of the decade. Its 'Theatrical Inspector' thought (or pretended to think) that *A Peep behind the Curtain* was by King, when it was really by Garrick. The review is therefore, amusingly oblique: 'I am very sorry that impartiality obliges me to arraign Mr. King at the bar of the public, as guilty of intruding a *bantling* of his own *brain* upon them; which, in the eye of genius, must be deemed a proof of his inability to write, and of the depraved taste of the town, who have suffered his piece to escape the rod of theatrical justice—damnation.'[44] The irony of the advice to King that as an actor he should stick to his last, was sharpened by the verdict that the farce was 'beneath the notice of the judicious.'

The notices did not confine themselves to new pieces but took in older plays as well and gave much space to the discussion of Tate's *King Lear* and Garrick's revisions of *Romeo and Juliet*. The magazine also performed a service to posterity by printing some engravings of scenes at the London theatres. The explanation of the second of them, Garrick as Abel Drugger, was delayed until the month after the plate had appeared, but then noted that the first and second figures on the left were Surly and Kastril, the Angry Boy. Opposite them the figure in the fighting attitude was Drugger, and to his right stood Ananias and Tribulation. 'The middlemost of the dark figures is Subtle.' Face stood at his right. The third plate showed a scene from Arthur Murphy's *The Citizen*, with Young Wilding beating Old Philpot, and Young Philpot and Maria watching aghast. The fourth engraving was of Barry and Mrs. Dancer as Lear and Cordelia in prison. All three give us a good idea of the theatrical

43 14 November 1767.   44 (1767), p. 612.   135

'attitudes' of the day.[45] Oil paintings of actors often appear to belong more to the studio than the playhouse, but these prints in their crudity and freshness, capture the excitement of performance.

With the seventies dramatic criticism in the reviews and newspapers became far more general. The feverish interest of the public in the stage forced them to carry some references to it in nearly every issue. Puffs and gossip were most frequently printed. Notices of new plays were quite often published immediately after the first performances and, though they were still largely summaries of the story, they also contained critical remarks of a reasonable standard. These were supplemented in succeeding issues by letters expressing agreement or disagreement, usually from interested parties.

Two newspapers were particularly important in their own way. The *Morning Post*, founded in 1772, soon gained a name for its scandalous gossip and waspish critiques. Its editor, the Rev. Henry Bate, may have been 'Scorpion', the writer of its stinging reviews, and was possibly satirised in 'Snake', the author and critic in *The School for Scandal*. At the other extreme, the *Morning Chronicle* achieved a reputation for honesty and integrity. Its editor from 1774 was William Woodfall, who had been an actor and tried to present all points of view concerning the stage.

Impartiality was certainly needed, for once periodicals were recognised as being influential enough to sway public opinion about the theatres, their editors and publishers were courted by everyone seeking favourable publicity for themselves, or hostile criticism of enemies.

Since comments, paragraphs and critiques, were all anonymous, people were sometimes suspicious of the writers' motives. The unsophisticated, however, assumed that everything in print was accurate, and had to be warned against accepting as fair comment what was really prejudiced. Samuel Foote educated his audience at the Haymarket by writing a prologue

[45] (1767), facing pp. 9, 113, 446. Here present on pp. 26, 142 and 44.

The School of Shakespear.

Dr. William Kendrick gives weekly lectures on Shakespeare.

in which Laconic and Snarl discussed the methods of a hack-writer for the newspapers. Snarl remarked, 'I know the tricks of your trade, the old plan of plaintiff and defendant; Theatricus condemns, Leonora defends, Buckhorse reviles, Tranquillus retorts; What the Director asserts, a Proprietor denies: Whilst, all the time, Theatricus, Leonora, Buckhorse, Tranquillus, the Director, and the Proprietor, all centre in one individual, call'd Timothy Snarl.'[46]

The proprietors of the playhouses were eager to prevent criticism of themselves and their undertakings, so *The Monitor* warned the public to be on its guard against their stifling of opposition to their plans: 'the coalition of the *Gazetteer* with the *Public Advertiser*, . . . the *St. James's Chronicle*, and other papers, whereby true criticism, public remarks, tyrannical complaints, and the check of the public, are at least impeded, if not attempted to be frustrated; are things which certainly should excite proper suspicions, and a new channel to be opened for introducing public right and public liberty over the theatres. 'Tis therefore presumed that the public will look on the above papers as partial and servile. . . . '[47] The cause of this complaint lay in the rough treatment meted out to Mr. and Mrs. Yates at Covent Garden and Drury Lane, and their inability to air their grievances because the newspapers were under the control of theatre managers and their hirelings.

This is accurate to a certain extent, but is not the whole truth. Some of the remarks made in the celebrated quarrel over the management of Covent Garden Theatre between George Colman and Thomas Harris, support the idea that some newspapers were venal. Harris accused Colman of filling them (and particularly 'your' *St James's Chronicle*) with 'libellous and unmanly insinuations.'[48] Colman retorted that Harris was 'continually running to all the news-printers in town with his own scurrilous letters and paragraphs, and his friend Mr.

46 *Universal Museum* (1767), 277. 47 (1767), p. 3.
48 *A Letter from T. Harris to G. Colman, on the Affairs of Covent Garden* (1768), p. 1.

Kenrick's dirty epigrams in his pocket; having . . . undertaken to pay a round price for their suffering their papers to become the registers of his falsehood, and journals of his malignity.'[49]

Garrick also came under attack for his connection with the newspapers. He had a twentieth share in the *St. James's Chronicle* (owned, among others, by Bonnell Thornton and George Colman), and his connection was obvious on 25 November 1765 when the publisher, Henry Baldwin, put out a statement of accounts and Garrick signed a receipt for £68. 2s. 6d., presumably his share of the profits.[50] We know for sure that he contributed a sketch of Preville to its columns in June 1765,[51] a critique of *The School for Scandal* to the issue of 8–10 May 1777, and an 'Ode to the Author of *The School for Scandal*' to that of 24–27 May. He may have written much more, and was accused of doing so by Francis Gentleman when he mentioned two evening papers that Garrick and Colman owned. Gentleman added, 'every defence of their impositions and absurdities, however vague, is greedily admitted; indeed we believe every thing favourable is written by themselves.' He also put the accusation into verse:

> The London Packet, the St. James's join
> To vend the puffs which I and Davy coin,[52]

The viperous William Kenrick was even more scathing, putting the following words in Garrick's mouth:

> Tho' Harry Woodfall, Baldwin, Evans, Say,
> My puffs in fairest order full display;
> Impartially insert each friendly PRO
> Suppressing every CON of every foe.[53]

We are asked to believe that Henry Sampson Woodfall, printer of the *Public Advertiser*, Thomas Evans, of the *London Packet*, and Charles Say, of *The Gazetteer*, were all as corrupt as Baldwin.

49 *T. Harris Dissected* (1768), p. 2.
50 Puttick and Sampson's sale catalogue, 19 February 1874, item 145.
51 *Letters of David Garrick, ed. cit.*, p. 463; and cf. 411, 559, 1020.
52 Sir Nicholas Nipclose, *The Theatres* (1772), p. 33.
53 *A Letter to David Garrick* (3rd ed., 1772), p. 16.

Kenrick then showed Garrick abusing newspapers that were free from taint:

> Curse on that Ledger[54] and that damn'd Whitehall,[55]
> How players and managers they daily maul!
> . . .
> Curse on that Morning-Chronicle; whose tale
> Is never known with spightful wit to fail.[56]

The fact is that Kenrick as much as Garrick or Colman was involved, anonymously, in the business of praise and abuse for personal ends.

Colman made a jest of the subject in *New Brooms*, a dialogue between Phelim and Catcall given at Drury Lane Theatre in September 1776. Phelim wanted to try his luck on the stage, and Catcall offered to help him by writing puffs. He boasted, 'The Town knows me well enough, and so do the Managers; I give them a touch now and again in the papers: *Dramaticus* in the Chronicle, the *Observer* in the Post, the *Elephant* in the Packet, the *Drury Lane Mouse* and *Covent Garden Cricket*—all mine Phelim.'[57]

Of these the most amusing is 'the Mouse in the Green Room', the pseudonym for the writer of paragraphs in the *Morning Chronicle* of 1776. Kitty Clive was sure that they were composed by Garrick, and wrote to him on 31 January to say, ' I *had* Read the Mouse in the green room; and I knew its face the Moment I saw it; *a pretty little black-eyed fellow*; it is most admirably done. They all truly deserve what I am sure they felt when they read it.'[58] Once the author's identity is revealed,[59] we are bound to wonder how far it was generally known, and whether or not Colman expected Garrick to be taken for Catcall by the audience. In the civil warfare of

---

54 *The Public Ledger.*
55 *The Whitehall Evening Post.*
56 *A Letter to David Garrick*, pp. 18–19.
57 *The London Packet*, 2–4 October 1776.
58 Folger Shakespeare Library MS. Y. c. 552 (5).
59 Cf. *The Letters of David Garrick (ed. cit.)*, pp. 1143, 1152.

theatres and newspapers, secrets were not long kept; but the answers to both questions remain uncertain.

The period was one in which 'interest' and 'party' prevailed everywhere, so it is to be expected that the managers exercised some control over periodicals dealing with the theatre. Yet Garrick himself was seldom pleased by the paragraphs concerning him in the *St. James's Chronicle*, and there is good reason to believe that the editor printed some adverse criticism to stir up controversy and sell the newspaper.

What was too often forgotten was that publicity, however artful and seductive, could rarely persuade people to attend plays that were known to be caviare to the general: Addison's *The Drummer* is an obvious example. On the other hand, a new piece that enthralled an audience drew crowds without the help of newspaper puffing. Only the play that was almost a success really required this kind of assistance.

King as Marplot in Mrs. Centlivre's *The Busy Body*.

CHAPTER EIGHT

Plays

The patent theatres presented different programmes every night of the week, and naturally had to depend on stock pieces for the bulk of the entertainment they provided. These were often given more than once during a season, usually with different afterpieces. To us it seems amazing that the same playgoers went there night after night, and were fairly contented with the arrangement. We must assume, from the evidence already quoted, that many attended merely to join fashionable company and others were there, like members of a twentieth-century audience at the opera, to hear again pieces they knew well, given different interpretations by different casts. There was undoubtedly a great interest in technique, yet grumbles were also heard from time to time about the lack of variety and novelty, in the repertoire.

The 'Theatrical Inspector' of the *Universal Museum* in 1767 noted 'the playhouses opened, Drury-Lane on the 12th of September, with the Clandestine Marriage, and Covent-Garden on the 14th, with the Rehearsal. They have, therefore performed 57 nights, including the 27th [November], when my reckoning ends. As the filling of the houses depends more upon stated visitors (who are fond of theatrical representations, and attend three or four times every week) than the adventitious succour of such as come but once or twice in a season, it is easy to determine to whom the managers are most accountable.

I am of that number, and cannot help passing a severe censure upon the rulers of either house, for being deficient in point of variety.' He went on to examine the programmes of the fifty-seven nights in some detail, and concluded, 'we have had at Drury-Lane thirty-four and at Covent Garden twenty-nine different plays, and joining both houses together, it cannot but raise our indignation to see that we have had only a variety of fifty-three.' He then turned to a consideration of the farces offered, and noted an even smaller choice: 'we have only sixteen different pieces at Drury-Lane, and the same number at Covent-Garden, as if they had contrived to incur . . . equal blame.'[1]

A careful analysis[2] has been made of the programmes given at the patent theatres between 1747 and 1776, and it reveals that the most frequently repeated piece was *The Beggar's Opera* (1727). The most popular tragedies were, in order, *Romeo and Juliet, Hamlet, Jane Shore, King Lear,* and *Macbeth.* Comedies most often presented were Cibber and Vanbrugh's *The Provok'd Husband* (1727), Farquhar's *The Beaux Stratagem* (1707), Hoadly's *The Suspicious Husband* (1747), Steele's *The Conscious Lovers* (1721), and Ben Jonson's *Every Man in his Humour.* The comedies are newer than the tragedies, but only one of them belongs to the middle of the eighteenth century.

The order of preference is secured by combining the figures available for the most popular plays at each patent theatre. If we keep them separate, we find that some pieces were much more frequently performed at one house than the other. Drury Lane audiences liked Congreve's *The Mourning Bride* (1697), Rowe's *The Fair Penitent* (1703), as well as Otway's *The Orphan* (1680) and *Venice Preserved* (1682). Covent Garden preferred Lee's *The Rival Queens* (1677) and Ambrose Philips's *The Distrest Mother* (1712). Favourite comedies at Drury Lane were *Much Ado about Nothing* and *Cymbeline, The Clandestine Marriage* (1766) and *The Provok'd Wife* (1697). Covent Garden liked *The Merry Wives*

---

1 Pp. 558–9.
2 *The London Stage*, 1747–1776 (ed. G. W. Stone), pp. clxii–clxv.

of Windsor and *The Merchant of Venice*, Fielding's adaptation, *The Miser* (1732) and Mrs. Centlivre's *The Busy Body* (1708). All these show a very conservative taste, and we ought to bear in mind when assessing it, a comment by the *London Chronicle* on *The Conscious Lovers*: it was 'not an admired piece with the multitude, but has always met with a favourable response from a sensible and polite audience.'[3] In other words, the pit and boxes appreciated it, but the galleries preferred more robust and newer entertainment.

The Citizen, Act.2.Scene.1. as performid at Covent-Garden Theatre by Mr. Shuter, Mr. Woodward & Mr. Dyer. Publish'd according to Act of Parliament. by J. Payne in Paternoster Row. March 31. 1767.

A lively scene from Arthur Murphy's play.

They found it in the afterpieces, though even among those, three favourites were old: Ravenscroft's *The Anatomist* (1697), Carey's *The Contrivances* (1715), and Coffey's *The Devil to Pay* (1731). The rest were more up to date. Garrick's *Miss in her*

[3] 5–7 November 1771.

Teens (1747), *Lethe* (1748) and *High Life below Stairs* (1759), were as successful at Drury Lane as Murphy's *The Upholsterer* (1758) and *The Citizen* (1761) were at Covent Garden. Farces and burlettas were not the only entertainments included in the category of afterpieces, for some short comedies were also written to fill out the programme at both houses. Drury Lane presented: Murphy's *The Old Maid* (1761), Foote's *The Lyar* (1764), Garrick's *A Peep behind the Curtain* (1767) and *The Irish Widow* (1772). At Covent Garden, Foote, and Colman were responsible for the most successful short comedies: the former for *The Englishman in Paris* (1753), *The Englishman Returned from Paris* (1756), and *The Commissary* (1765); and Colman for *The Oxonian in Town* (1770) and *Man and Wife* (1770).[4] Not one of these plays was equally popular at both houses, because they tended to be confined to the theatre where each had been first played.

Some older comedies and afterpieces received new life when they were brought out in altered form. This was true of Restoration pieces that had to be toned down, and Garrick emphasised the point in a prologue he wrote for Sheridan's revision of Vanbrugh's *The Relapse* (1697), now called *A Trip to Scarborough*:

> As change thus circulates throughout the nation,
> Some plays may justly call for alteration;
> At least to draw some slender cov'ring o'er
> That graceless wit, which was too bare before:
> Those writers well and wisely use their pens,
> Who turn our Wantons into Magdalens.

Sheridan makes his own attitude clear in a speech by one of the characters in the revised version: 'we should preserve all we can of our deceased authors, at least till they are outdone by the living ones.' He eliminated anything that could give offence, but retained, almost in their entirety, the racy comic scenes. Other writers completely transformed certain earlier plays. The

4 *The London Stage*, 1747–1776 (ed. G. W. Stone, Jr.), p. clxvii.

most obvious example of this process was Garrick's adaptation of Wycherley's *The Country Wife* (1675) as *The Country Girl* (1766), when a cynical and robust comedy became a charming trifle.

Shakespeare's plays were also revised. Dramatists of the Restoration and early eighteenth century had altered a number of them to suit the taste of the age, but Garrick and his contemporaries cut out much of this material, restored many lines from the original, and sometimes gave the plays a more 'regular' form.

King Lear provides an interesting illustration. Nahum Tate's version held the stage for a century and a half after its first performance in 1681, and was generally preferred to Shakespeare's own text. Dr. Johnson thought that common opinion in this matter was all important and wrote: 'the public has decided. Cordelia, from the time of Tate, has always retired with victory and felicity. And, if my sensations could add any thing to the general suffrage, I might relate, I was many years ago so shocked by Cordelia's death, that I know not whether I ever endured to read again the last scenes of the play till I undertook to revise them as an editor.'[5]

In Tate's version, poetic justice was not only done but was seen to be done. Goneril and Regan were poisoned off; Edgar and Cordelia were married; Lear took over his throne again. The Fool was left out, for he had no place in a world of such happy regularity. When Samuel Foote saw Garrick in this adaptation in 1747, he advised him to read Shakespeare's original again 'and then make the Public and the Memory of the Author some amends by giving *Lear* in the *Original, Fool* and all.'[6] Garrick responded in part in October 1756, when he presented a text[7] that replaced much of Tate's paraphrasing

[5] S. Johnson, *Works* (1820), ii. 165.
[6] *An Examen of the New Comedy Call'd The Suspicious Husband* (1747), p. 35.
[7] G. W. Stone, Jr., points out in 'Garrick's production of *King Lear*', *Studies in Philology*, xlv (1948), 96, that this is probably represented in Bell's editions of Shakespeare's plays in 1773 and 1774, but that they include fewer lines of Shakespeare than the edition published in 1786 by C. Bathurst, as 'Altered from Shakespear by David Garrick, Esq.'

with Shakespeare's original lines: for example, Edmund's speech on his own bastardy was very properly restored. Yet the Fool was still excluded and Gloucester's blinding was reported, not seen.

Colman's version of the tragedy (presented at Covent Garden on 20 February 1768) went much further in the direction of reform. The love affair between Edgar and Cordelia was deleted because the ragged Edgar seemed a ludicrous lover and the whole episode was not likely to increase pathos. Gloucester's notion that he had fallen over Dover cliff was omitted as quite improbable, and Colman toyed with the idea of bringing back the Fool. He did not do so for a very good reason: 'such a character in Tragedy would not be endured on the modern stage.' Curiously enough, his whole adaptation could not be endured, and it failed completely. The alterations robbed the play of its normal appeal to sensibility. Colman had gone too far, too fast.

This was the kind of mistake Garrick seldom made. He was anxious to bring back Shakespeare's lines to the public stage but not at the expense of a 'strong' situation. This is clear from his alteration of *Macbeth*. Davenant's version was current for seventy years after its printing in 1674, and it presents Lady Macduff as a highly virtuous woman, wholly opposed to worldly ambition and offering a great contrast to Lady Macbeth. It used music and songs and (so that the witches might fly) machines. Garrick's version (7 January 1744) cut out over two hundred of Davenant's lines, but still followed him in retaining the dancing witches and omitting the drunken porter. Since Shakespeare's ending of the play appeared to Garrick a little tame, he added a speech[8] for the dying Macbeth:

> 'Tis done, the scene of life will quickly close.
> Ambition's vain, delusive dreams are fled,
> And now I wake to darkness, guilt and horror.
> I cannot bear it! let me shake it off—

8 See K. Burnim, *David Garrick, Director* (Pittsburgh, 1961), pp. 123–5, for the way in which Garrick leads up to this speech.

'Two' not be; my soul is clogg'd with blood—
I cannot rise! I dare not ask for mercy—
It is too late, hell drags me down. I sink
I sink—oh!—my soul is lost forever! [*Dies*]

To the reader this is melodramatic; to the leading actor, a last opportunity for the display of passionate feeling. By any standard the lines are meretricious.

Garrick used rather similar methods in his version of *Romeo and Juliet*. Romeo's love for Rosaline is not mentioned in the two earlier versions, Otway's *Caius Marius* (1680) and Theophilus Cibber's *Romeo and Juliet* (1744), and Garrick omits it too. Romeo and Juliet do not now meet for the first time at the dance in the house of the Capulets. Garrick also followed Otway in allowing Juliet to return to consciousness in the tomb before Romeo died, and wrote sixty-five lines of his own to fill up the scene. They end:

Juliet And did I wake for this?
Romeo   My powers are blasted,
    'Twixt death and love I am torn—I am distracted!
    But death's strongest—and must I leave thee, *Juliet!*
    O cruel, cursed fate: in sight of heav'n!
Juliet Thou rav'st—lean on my breast—
Romeo Fathers have flinty hearts, no tears can melt 'em.
    Nature pleads in vain—Children must be wretched.
Juliet O my breaking heart—
Romeo She is my wife—our hearts are twin'd together,
    Capulet forbear—*Paris*, loose your hold—
    Pull not our heart strings thus—they crack—they break—
    Oh *Juliet, Juliet!*   [*Dies*][9]

Garrick's version held the stage for over a hundred years, and was thought superb by some of his contemporaries. An interesting comment of this kind is to be found in the *London Chronicle* of 12–15 February 1757: 'There is Reason to think Shakespeare was not Master of the Italian Language, as it appears that the

[9] See G. C. D. Odell, *Shakespeare from Betterton to Irving* (1921), I. 343–7, for a full account.

Circumstance of Juliet's awaking before Romeo's death is omitted in a Translation of the Novel, to be seen in the Court of Pleasure. Had Shakespeare seen the Original, he would never have omitted such a fine dramatic incident. Otway has perceived this omission, and in his *Caius Marius* has taken advantage of so beautiful a Circumstance. But we cannot help agreeing with Mr. Garrick in his Preface, to the Play as it now stands, that it is surprizing such a Genius as Otway has not struck out a Scene of more Nature, Terror, and Distress. He who generally spoke the Language of the Heart, has, in this Instance, given us nothing but unaffecting Conceits, which can never agitate the Passions, as was proved some Winters ago, when Mr. Sheridan attempted to restore Otway's lines, amidst the general Hissing of the whole House.[10] The Scene, as it now stands, is written by Mr. Garrick, and has not an Idea, or Expression through the whole which is found ineffectual; so well has he judged of the natural Force of unornamented Dialogue in Distress.'

The same newspaper was much less enthusiastic about Garrick's adaptation of *The Winter's Tale*. He had drastically cut the play from five to three acts and concentrated interest on the sheep-shearing, transferring many of Shakespeare's best passages to it, but also adding new lines for Autolycus and some explanatory material. The main complaint by the *London Chronicle* concerned the scene of the discovery of Hermione, which was disliked for very good eighteenth-century reasons: 'her having lived sequestered for many years might be allowed, if she did not stand for a statue at the last. This Circumstance is certainly childish, as is likewise the pretended revival of her by musick. Had Hermione been discovered to us in a rational manner, the Close would have been pathetic, whereas at present, notwithstanding many strokes of fine writing, Reason operates too strongly against the Incident, and our Passions subside into Calmness and Inactivity.'[11]

10 Thomas Sheridan played Romeo at Covent Garden on 20 November and 26 December 1754.   11 24–26 March 1757.

Garrick's adaptation of *Hamlet* met with an equally guarded response. He mentioned the revision in a letter of 3 January 1773; 'I have ventur'd to alter Hamlet, & have greatly Succeeded; I have destroy'd the Grave diggers, (those favourites of the people) & almost all of the 5th Act—it was a bold Deed'.[12] The boldness lay partly in the exclusion of the duel and the grave-diggers, and partly in the new ending that he wrote. Gertrude ran off the stage, and fell into a trance under her 'Load of Agony and Sorrow.' In his dying speeches, Hamlet hoped that she would repent, and in his last breath made provision for the Kingdom:

> . . . but one thing more,
> O take this hand from me—unite your Virtues—
> (*joins Horatio's hand to Laertes'*)
> To claim this troubled hand—I can no more
> Nor have I more to ask but Mercy Heav'n. (*Dies*)[13]

Sensibility permited Gertrude (like Cordelia) to suffer but not die. Duty required Hamlet to stab Claudius and fall upon Laertes's sword:

> 'tis the Hand of Heav'n
> Administers by him this precious balm
> For all my Wounds.

Performances of this version held the stage for the remaining three years of Garrick's management, but when he retired, audiences favoured a return to the grave-diggers and the duel.

He was no luckier when he attempted to rescue *Antony and Cleopatra* from the study. He put on Capell's adaptation of it at Drury Lane on 3 January 1759, and the audience saw a tactful effort to give new theatrical life to a literary masterpiece. The action in general and the allusions to the politics of the ancient world, were simplified. The leading characters were filled out a little, and the lesser ones cut down or eliminated. The final

---

12 *The Letters of David Garrick* (ed. D. M. Little and G. M. Kahrl, Cambridge, Mass., 1963), ii. 840.

13 G. W. Stone, Jr., 'Garrick's Long Lost Alteration of *Hamlet*,' *Publications of the Modern Language Association of America*, xlix (1934), 890–921.

achievement was interesting, and though Garrick himself lacked a commanding presence as Antony and was not greatly attracted to the part, he was quite well supported by Mrs. Yates as Cleopatra. The novelty met with increasing applause in the theatre and some hostility from the critics. After six nights it was taken off, never to be revived again during Garrick's management.[14] He excused the failure by noting that he had suffered from colic and had felt weak.

A number of other adaptations of Shakespeare's plays were made during this period, and the variety of treatment given them may be seen by comparing *Cymbeline* with *The Taming of the Shrew*. On 28 November 1761, Garrick presented *Cymbeline* 'with many fine Passages omitted', but very few real alterations. Nevertheless a play of this kind must lose much of its beauty when any of its poetic effect is taken away. This objection cannot be applied with equal force to *The Taming of the Shrew*, where the action rather than the poetry, gives delight. Garrick stripped it down to become a well-made farce called *Catherine and Petruchio*, that held a place in the theatre till 1886.

There were critics who disapproved of adaptations of any kind because they were really old plays that prevented possible eighteenth-century masterpieces from being given. The point of view is clearly expressed by Goldsmith:

What must be done? only sit down contented, cry up all that comes before us, and admire even the absurdities of Shakespeare. Let the reader suspend his censure; I admire the beauties of this great father of our stage as much as they deserve, but could wish, for the honour of our country, and for his honour too, that many of his scenes were forgotten. . . . Let the spectator who assists at any of these new revived pieces, only ask himself, whether he would approve such a performance if written by a modern poet; if he would not, then his applause proceeds merely from the sound of a name and an empty veneration for antiquity. In fact, the revival of those pieces of forced humour, far fetch'd conceit, and unnatural hyper-

---

14 See G. W. Stone, Jr., 'Garrick's Presentation of *Antony and Cleopatra*,' *Review of English Studies*, xiii (1937), 20–38.

bole, which have been ascribed to Shakespear, is rather gibbeting than raising a statue to his memory; it is rather a trick of the actor, who thinks it safest acting in exaggerated characters, and who by out-stepping nature, chuses to exhibit the ridiculous outré of an harlequin under the sanction of this venerable name.[15]

The real point that Goldsmith wishes to stress comes in his next paragraph, when he says, 'No matter what the play may be, it is the actor who draws an audience.' He adds, 'the spectator, in a fool's paradise, knows not what all this means till the last act concludes in matrimony. The piece pleases our critics, because it talks old English; and it pleases the galleries because it has fun. True taste, or even common sense are out of the question.'[16] Goldsmith implied that Garrick's revivals of Shakespeare's plays were partly for the sake of self-aggrandisement, an idea that struck people more forcibly ten years later, when Garrick put on 'The Stratford Jubilee.' He also suggested that the manager preferred these revivals because he did not have to pay the author: 'I am not insensible that third nights[17] are disagreeable drawbacks upon the annual profits of the stage.'

He extended his argument by mentioning that he had heard 'no new play can be admitted upon our theatre unless the author chuses to wait some years', and even that implied 'courting the manager as well as the muse.' What he also required was 'adulation to please his vanity, powerful patrons to support their merit, or money to indemnify disappointment.'[18]

Other writers repeat these complaints throughout the period about the difficulty of getting their plays acted. The anonymous author of *A Letter to Mr. Garrick on his having purchased the Patent* declared that 'the Public was deprived of a very excellent Tragedy, wrote by one of our best Dramatic Authors, and designed to have been exhibited last Winter, & he will find it was because a certain great *Actor* did not like the Part allotted for him, not because it was not a good one, but because it was

15 Goldsmith, *Collected Works* (ed. Friedman), i. 326.   16 *Ibid.*, i. 327.
17 See p. 15 above, and p. 153.   18 *Ibid.*, 1. 327–8.

not the *only* good one.'[19] Theophilus Cibber grumbled, 'unless a Play comes strongly recommended from some high Interest, how difficult is it to get it read? . . . to gain Admittance to them [Managers] is frequently more difficult, than to come at a Prime Minister.'[20] In 1759, the following passage was to be found in an open letter to Garrick: 'You have now been above Ten years manager, and in the course of that period you have favoured the public with about six or eight new pieces, besides your own works and retouches, and Mr. Woodward's pantomimes: and within the same time you have rejected upwards of six score.'[21] In 1767, too, a similar charge was made: 'Mr. G——— perhaps from a motive of jealousy, as he is an author himself, has always done his utmost to depress dramatic authors and cut down unfledged merit. When Mr. Murphy first offered him his Orphan of China, he for a long time would not suffer it to be acted.[22]

A writer in the mid-eighteenth century was peculiarly unlucky in the few openings that existed for new plays. For most of the year only two theatres were active and able to accept his offerings, but their system of constantly presenting favourite plays of the past left them small opportunity for including new works. Authors like Bickerstaff might enjoy reasonable security for a time as house-playwrights, but the rest had little certainty of acceptance. They persevered because a successful dramatist achieved immediate fame and useful financial rewards. He drew the takings (less expenses) of the third, sixth, and ninth nights of production, and could also expect a hundred pounds from the sale of his copyright to a publisher. The distribution of the printed play also helped to make his name widely known, for at this period plays were more popular reading than novels. For example, William Bathoe's *New Catalogue* of his London circulating library in 1757, revealed that fiction

19 (?1747), p. 16.
20 *Two Dissertations on the Theatres* (1756), p. 29.
21 *A Letter to the Author of The Rout* (1759), p. 21.
22 *The Monitor,* 7 November 1767, p. 7.

L

formed a tenth and plays nearly a third of 4735 works listed.[23]

Some figures are available to show how difficult it was to get a new play produced. In the thirty-five seasons between 1741 and 1776, only seventy new mainpieces were presented at Drury Lane, and fifty-four at Covent Garden. Separate figures for afterpieces show that at Drury Lane one hundred and eighteen were given over the same period, an average of just over three a year.[24] Garrick appears to have been a little more willing to promote new plays than the various managers of Covent Garden, but the number presented at both houses was very small.

It is worth examining a sample of them, beginning with tragedies. One of the problems that managers had to face was that learned men were encouraged to think that their intimate knowledge of Greek drama fitted them to write tragedies that would move playgoers profoundly. They duly wrote works that were full of moral elevation and high-sounding sentiments:

> Fiction was then the physic of the mind,
> The passions purg'd, and sentiments refin'd.
> Dramatic works to sermons were ally'd,
> And theatres by pulpits sanctify'd.[25]

They had a good knowledge of the theory of heroic drama, but little stage experience. Their eloquence was often unpoetic. A few of their tragedies were successful for a short time, others were immediately damned, and others were never acted. Yet the authors all hoped that their genius would be recognised at last, as is evident in the case of a fellow-sufferer in the cause of virtue and literature: 'Died the noted Chevalier Descalzeaux, who resided for thirty Years in a Garret within the Rules of the

23 Paul Kaufman, 'The Reading of Plays in the Eighteenth Century,' *Bulletin of the New York Public Library*, liii (1969), 566.
24 I have obtained these figures by adding together those presented in *The London Stage*, Pt. 3 (ed. A. H. Scouten), p. cliii, and Pt. 4 (ed. G. W. Stone, Jr.), p. clxix. Figures for afterpieces at Covent Garden are not available.
25 F.B.L., *The Rational Rosciad* (1787), p. 2.

Fleet. He has left by his Will, his Tragedy of Turnus. between the Managers of our Theatres, and the King of France.'[26]

All the tragedies I have chosen were well known for one reason or another: Johnson's Irene (1749), Home's *Douglas* (1756), Dodsley's *Cleone* (1758), and Murphy's *The Orphan of China* (1759).

Irene is remembered because of Samuel Johnson's eminence in other fields. The theme was taken from Knolles's *Generall Historie of the Turkes* (1603), and most of the tragedy appears to have been written at Edial in March 1737 before Johnson left for London with his pupil, David Garrick. He received no encouragement from the patent theatres until Garrick became joint manager of Drury Lane ten years later. Johnson re-wrote the work and it was presented there, as *Mahomet and Irene*, on 6 February 1749. The long wait was typical, but the author's reward was rather better than usual. Garrick provided the play with lavish costumes, and took part in it himself, with Barry, Mrs. Pritchard and Mrs. Cibber. Because of his efforts, it ran for nine nights, and brought the author £195 from the takings, and £100 from the sale of the copyright. It was never revived.

The prologue promised a great theme:

> Our daring bard with spirit unconfin'd,
> Spreads wide the mighty moral for mankind.
> Learn here how Heav'n supports the virtuous mind.

The aim is Miltonic, but the blank verse does not rise to great heights. A tragedy that is so sluggish in its action, should be vivid in its phrasing, but Johnson fails to stir the listener. As Boswell noted,[27] the play contains 'a rich store of noble sentiments . . . ; but it is deficient in pathos, in that delicate power of touching the human feelings.' Mustapha notes Cali's 'sorcery of tongue' but this is not really evident in the Vizier's speeches, and Mahomet has some better lines:

> Now let him go pursu'd by silent wrath,

26 *Felix Farley's Bristol Journal*, 29 February 1772.
27 *Life of Johnson* (ed. G. B. Hill, rev. L. F. Powell, Oxford, 1934), i. 198.

> Meet unexpected daggers in his way
> And in some distant land obscurely die. (II. iv)

Occasionally he is bombastic: Gibbon noted some extravagance of language and allusion, when pointing out that 'Mahomet's passion soars above sense and reason.'[28] Like his *Irene*, Johnson manages to 'exhaust the stores of pious eloquence', and the patience of his audience.

Garrick attempted to give the tragedy a more forceful climax by arranging for *Irene* to be strangled with a Turkish bowstring in full sight of the spectators, but this was so badly received that at subsequent performances, she was despatched off-stage. Whether the protest was caused by the shock of seeing outrageous violence or by Garrick's forgetting the classical rules, is uncertain.

The other three tragedies I shall discuss were all rejected by Garrick. John Home's *Douglas* had the backing of the Earl of Bute, but the great actor reported on 10 July 1756 that the first two acts were tedious, the development of the plot improbable, the language 'too often below the most familiar Dialogue'. He concluded that it was so radically defective that it would never raise the passions.[29] Home sent it to the Edinburgh Theatre and, on 14 December, it was so successfully produced there that Covent Garden put it on exactly three months later. The *London Chronicle* commented: 'From the opening of the Play, we felt our Passions irresistibly seized and attached to the Subject; Mrs. Woffington, who begins it, breaks into a beautiful Pathos, at once poetical and simple.' It added, 'the Catastrophe is very affecting: Hope, Joy, Terror, and Pity . . . were here agitated to a very high degree of Emotion.' A later issue mentioned some 'exquisitely tender scenes' and the 'beautiful simplicity' of the whole composition.[30] Thomas Gray noted infinite faults, but

---

28 Johnson, *Poems* (ed. E. L. McAdam, Jr., with George Milne, New Haven and London, 1964), p. 143, quoting *The Decline and Fall of the Roman Empire* (1788), vi. 494.
29 *The Letters of David Garrick (ed. cit.,)* i. 245–6.
30 12–15, 15–17 March 1757.

thought the author had 'retrieved the true language of the stage, which had been lost for these hundred years.'[31] This is not very apparent now, but other writers were struck by Home's mastery of words. Goldsmith gave a qualified judgement on the play, but praised the scenes of rural simplicity: 'the native innocence of the shepherd Norval, is happily expressed; it requires some art to dress the thoughts and phrases of the common people, without letting them swell into bombast, or sink into vulgarity, a fault generally charged upon the English Authors.'[32]

Garrick's criticism of the play's improbabilities and Goldsmith's suggestion that it was short of incidents, are still valid. The latter's belief that it lacked poetic fire was not shared by his contemporaries. This romantic tragedy contained two roles, Lady Randolph and Young Norval, that were to move audiences to a tumult of emotion for the next seventy years. In particular, Lady Randloph's excitement at recognising her long-lost son and her suicide when Lord Randolph jealously killed the youthful stranger, drew many a tear.

Dodsley's domestic tragedy, *Cleone*, also provided a noble and highly sympathetic role for a leading actress. The play had been long in the making, and Pope had advised the author to extend it to five acts. Shenstone, another poet, had read it in July 1756 and had been impressed by its 'extraordinary merit.' Garrick rejected it, possibly because the part offered him was too small, but Dodsley hoped he would relent, and revised the play again. Chesterfield was impressed by it and supported an application to Rich at Covent Garden. After some delay, it was performed there on 2 December 1758, with Mrs. Bellamy as Cleone.[33]

Even if the language is sometimes pedestrian, the plot is a good one and the first three acts grip the attention more than any other tragic scenes of the period. Glanville is a villain who

---

31 *Biographia Dramatica* (ed. Baker, rev. I. Reed, 1782), ii. 93.
32 *Collected Works (ed. cit.)*, i. 12.
33 R. Straus, *Robert Dodsley* (1910), pp. 205–6, 211, 218–25.

PLAYS

spreads slander about the general's wife, Cleone, until she takes refuge in the forest, where his assistant sets about murdering her and her child. She is only stunned but suddenly comes to herself:

Falls down by her child, kissing it and weeping. Then raising herself on her arm, after a dead silence and looking by degrees more and more wild, she proceeds in a distracted manner.

> Hark! hark! lie still, my love!—For all the world
> Don't stir!—'Tis Glanville and he'll murder us!
> Stay, stay—I'll cover thee with boughs—don't fear—
> I'll call the little lambs, and they shall bring
> Their softest fleece to shelter thee from cold.
> There, there—lie close—he shall not see—no, no;
> I'll tell him 'tis an angel I have hid. [*She rises up*]
> Where is he? soft!—he's gone, he's gone, my love,
> And shall not murder thee.—Poor innocent!
> 'Tis fast asleep. Well thought! I'll steal away,
> Now while he slumbers—pick wild berries for him,
> And bring a little water in my hand—
> Then, when he wakes, we'll seat us on the bank,
> And sing all night.

The pathos of the situation is strongly felt. After this point, the plot is more predictable. Glanville's machinations are discovered, and Cleone comes to her senses again just before her death. Her last words are less interesting, but to a generation that had wept over the lengthy tribulations of Clarissa Harlowe they had their appeal. A letter-writer in the *Public Advertiser* spoke of 'enjoying the most refined and human Pleasure, and by which we approach nearest to Divinity, to wit, that of shedding Tears for the misfortunes of others.' The tragedy 'breathes throughout but the purest morality, & that must have flowed from a thoroughly honest heart.'[34] Dodsley's sincerity was obvious to all. His skill was also apparent.

Murphy's *The Orphan of China* is interesting for different reasons: it is an adaptation of Voltaire's tragedy with the same

158   [34] Quoted by R. Straus, *op. cit.*, p. 231.

title, and also reminds us of the fashion for things Chinese at this period. Its novelty of setting led William Whitehead to remark in the prologue:

> Enough of Greece and Rome. Th'exhausted store
> Of either nation now can charm no more.

Garrick rejected the play twice, then agreed to refer it for critical analysis to Whitehead, poet-laureate and author of the tragedies, *Creusa* and *The Roman Father*. The critique was a long one, but seems to have persuaded Garrick to produce *The Orphan of China*. His next dilemma concerned his part: in a fortnight, he moved from Hamet to Zaphimri, and on to Zamti. A play that provided three parts which attracted Garrick deserved success, and when it was presented on 25 February 1759, it drew much applause. Some of the scenery designed for *The Chinese Festival* contributed to the tragedy's splendour, and Garrick was 'inimitable in Zamti; in nothing he had ever performed was he greater, except in King Lear.'[35]

Goldsmith was present at the first night and reported that 'the whole house seemed pleased, highly and justly pleased, but it was not with the *luxury of woe* they seemed affected: the nervous sentiment, the glowing imagery, the well-conducted scenery, seemed the sources of their pleasure: their judgment could not avoid approving the conduct of the drama, yet few of the situations were capable of getting within the soul, or exciting a single tear.'[36] He felt that pathos was aroused at the very start but without 'a proper preparation of incident' and that it was not 'in the power of genius to keep our sorrows alive through five acts, unless it diversifies the object.'

The focus of our attention is Zamti, a mandarin, and his wife Mandane, whose son Hamet is to be a sacrifice because Timurkan, the barbarian tyrant, believes him to be the young prince. The plot contains a number of emotional situations written in an exclamatory style and with prayers for strength,

---

35 J. Foot, *The Life of Arthur Murphy, Esq.* (1811), pp. 143–55.
36 *Collected Works (ed. cit.)*, i. 173.

invocations, and the customary conflict between love and duty. Some of the speeches are much too long but they include an unusual, revolutionary one by Zamti before Timurkan:

> Thy will
> The law in China!—Ill-instructed man!
> Now learn an awful truth,—Tho' ruffian pow'r
> May for a while suppress all sacred order,
> And trample on the rights of man;—the soul,
> Which gave our legislation life and vigour,
> Shall still subsist—above the tyrant's reach.—
> —The spirit of the laws can never die.

Timurkan feels the pangs of conscience before he is killed by the young prince. Mandane commits suicide not knowing she is about to be rescued.

Murphy said that he drew only in crayons and had no access to the lasting colours of the imagination. Posterity has agreed with him. His plotting and characterisation are effective and Goldsmith noted a justness of sentiment not to be found in Voltaire's version, but Murphy's attempt at elevation failed. He aimed at the sublime but became wordy and exclamatory.

This was a general fault of eighteenth-century writers of tragedy and they were not helped by the fashionable, over-weight, latinised diction. Many of their plays were tedious and deserved the rebuke administered as an 'Extempore on seeing Hoole's Tragedy of Cyrus':[37]

> Master Hoole
> Thou'rt not a fool:
> But do not tire us
> More with Cyrus.

The temper of the age may have militated against tragedy. Pathetic heroines were more popular than tragic heroes (other than Shakespeare's), and audiences were strongly moved by helpless innocence, loyal but distracted wives, and distressed mothers. But what the period really lacked was one playwright

37 *The Muse's Mirrour* (1778), i. 10.

with a genius for tragedy, who could turn all these disadvantages to account, produce great works of art and influence every writer of his time.

The tearfulness that was to be found in many a tragedy was caused by the mid-eighteenth century emphasis on delicacy and sensibility. These were to be found in comedy too.

This is apparent in plays like Kelly's *False Delicacy* (1768) and Cumberland's *The West Indian* (1771), two of the most successful comedies of the period. The very first lines of *False Delicacy* tell us that Lady Betty Lambton's refusal of Lord Winworth's offer of marriage 'was infinitely more the result of an extraordinary delicacy, than the want of affection for your Lordship.' Winworth therefore decides to woo Miss Marchmont who also possesses 'an uncommon share of delicacy, and may possibly think herself insulted by the offer of a rejected heart.' Delicacy therefore seems to be another name for sensitivity, disinterestedness, and even quixotry. Kelly was aware that fine feeling was much applauded in his day and could be admirable in a refined society, but that it could also be taken to ludicrous lengths. So he complicates his plot by showing that Miss Marchmont is in love with Sidney, but will marry Winworth out of a mistaken sense of obligation to Lady Betty. Sidney is expected to marry Miss Rivers, but she secretly prefers Sir Harry Newburg. They are people of 'a nice behaviour' foolish in their excess of scrupulousness, and well deserving Mrs. Harley's comment, 'The devil take this delicacy: I don't know anything it does besides making people miserable.' She stands for good sense, and serves to bring them all down to earth. They justify themselves in platitudes of a didactic kind that came to typify this sort of comedy.

The sentimental at an extreme may be noted in the longest speech of the play, in which the 'poor orphan', Miss Marchmont, looks back on her past history:

My life was mark'd out early by calamity,—and the first light I beheld was purchas'd with the loss of a mother.—The grave snatch'd away the best of fathers just as I came to know the value of such a blessing;—and hadn't it been for the exalted goodness of others, I, who once experienc'd the unspeakable pleasure of relieving the necessitous, had myself, perhaps, felt the immediate want of bread;—and shall I ungratefully sting the bosom which has thus benevolently cherished me?—Shall I basely wound the peace of those who have rescu'd me from despair,—and stab at their tranquillity in the very moment they honour me with protection? ... they deserve every sacrifice which I can make.—May the benignant hand of Providence shower endless happiness upon their heads, and may the sweets of a still-encreasing felicity be their portion, whatever becomes of me!

This is no worse than speeches of the same kind in Dickens but it is a pity that, for a hundred years, collections of clichés should have been accepted as the normal language of virtuous people in their moments of heartfelt emotion. Yet audiences and readers accepted them warmly, and wept at their generosity of spirit.

At the same time, we can see that Kelly wants to suggest that these kindly and well-meaning characters lack insight and, in terms of their own good, are rather foolish. The more sensible attitudes of Mrs. Harley and Mr. Cecil are contrasted with them, as in the instance when Mrs. Harley says of Miss Marchmont, 'Now will I be hang'd if she does not undo everything by a fresh stroke of delicacy.' The over-refined are blunderers. The idea is repeated in a quietly amusing scene (II. 2), when Winworth comes to Lady Betty's and appears to her to be about to make her a proposal. She responds warily but becomes more enthusiastic as he goes on, and is really astonished when he suddenly makes plain that he is asking Lady Betty for support in his wooing of Miss Marchmont.

Kelly's dialogue is suitably spirited when it comes from the lips of people lacking in delicacy, and a similar vigour is to be found in the lines given to Cumberland's Belcour and O'Flaherty in *The West Indian*. Belcour has been brought up in the West Indies and is shown as ingenuous but hot-blooded, 'no match for the cunning and contrivances of this intriguing town',

London. He is deceived into thinking that Louisa Dudley is a woman of the streets and bluntly says to her, 'you are welcome to partake my fortune, give me in return your person, give me pleasure, give me love; free, unencumbered, anti-matrimonial love.' In a phrase that inevitably reminds us of nineteenth-century melodrama, she cries, 'Unhand me, sir!', and is rescued by her brother. Eventually Belcour's courage and honesty earn him forgiveness, and Louisa marries him.

Cumberland said later[38] that characters like Belcour and O'Flaherty were 'usually exhibited on the stage, as the butts for ridicule and abuse.' but that he had endeavoured 'to present them in such lights, as might tend to reconcile the world to them.' He succeeded, for Belcour was well liked and O'Flaherty (played by Moody) 'filled the theatre with repeated convulsions of laughter.'[39] He had been a soldier of fortune, who served in many armies but 'never knew what it was they were scuffling about.' He breaks off his wooing of Lady Rusport once he finds that she will not help Captain Dudley, and he remarks sagely, 'there isn't in the whole creation as savage an animal as a human creature without pity.' The stage Irishman of the day is given to 'bulls' and O'Flaherty is no exception: he says of the prospective duellists, 'Can't you settle your differences first, and dispute about 'em afterwards.' He is also an important figure in the plot since he can see that Lady Rusport and her lawyer are up to mischief. So he stands behind a screen and overhears them conspiring to deprive Charles Rusport of the estate left him by his grandfather. The lively O'Flaherty is always at hand at the right moment, and undoubtedly contributes much to the play's success.

The rest of the characters are less interesting. Lady Rusport and the Fulmers are obnoxious; the virtuous people are rather undistinguished and their lines are sometimes absurd in their sententiousness. For example, Charlotte is so struck by Belcour's generosity that she exclaims, 'O blessed be the torrid zone for ever, whose rapid vegetation quickens nature with such

38 *Memoirs* (1807), i. 274.   39 *Critical Review*, xxxi (1771), 113.   163

benignity.' The exclamatory manner seems equally silly in the recognition scene:

Stockwell: I am your father.
Belcour: My father! Do I live?
Stockwell: I am your father.
Belcour: It is too much; my happiness o'erpowers me; to gain a friend and find a father is too much; I blush to think how little I deserve you. (*They embrace.*)

But Major O'Flaherty brings them back to reality when he says, 'O my conscience, I think we shall be all related by and by.'

The author's sentimentality comes out most clearly when a will is found that leaves everything to the virtuous Charles and Louisa. She cries, 'Instruct me to support this unexpected turn of fortune', but Captain Dudley reproves her: 'Name not fortune; 'tis the work of Providence, 'tis the justice of Heaven that would not suffer innocence to be oppressed, nor your base aunt to prosper in her cruelty and cunning' (V. 6). Virtue is not in itself a sufficient reward.

Sentimental comedy, then, had its moments of humour and of satiric force, and it remains a question whether the excellent audiences these two plays drew, were more attracted by the fun or the moralising. In his famous 'Comparison between Laughing and Sentimental Comedy', Goldsmith showed that he knew the correct answer. Sentimental drama belonged to a 'species of Bastard Tragedy', in which 'the virtues of Private Life are exhibited, rather than the Vices exposed; and the Distresses, rather than the Faults of Mankind, make our interest in the piece.'[40] He remarked too that it offered only insipid dialogue, and that humour seemed to be departing from the stage.

The essay was printed in 1773, and in the previous thirty years, only three celebrated 'laughing comedies' had been written: Hoadly's *The Suspicious Husband* (1747), Colman's *The Jealous Wife* (1761), and Colman and Garrick's *The Clandestine*

[40] *Collected Works* (ed. cit.), iii. 212–13.

Marriage (1766). In the four years after Goldsmith's critique was published, another three delightful comedies appeared: *She Stoops to Conquer* (1773), *The Rivals* (1775), and *The School for Scandal* (1777). His words and his play seem to have had a revivifying effect.

The earlier title of *The Suspicious Husband* was 'The Rake',[41] and in many ways it was the better one. It describes accurately Ranger's character in the first half of the play, even if in the later part he becomes more of the lively man of feeling. The contrast is made clear in a perceptive judgement by Samuel Foote: 'His Errors arise from the Want of Reflection; a lively Imagination, with a great flow of Spirits, hurries him into all the fashionable Follies of the Town; but throw the least shadow of Wickedness or Dishonour on an Action, and he avoids it with the same Care that he would a Precipice.'[42] The part suited Garrick splendidly. By contrast, Strictland, the suspicious husband, remains a very unsympathetic character throughout: his jealousy becomes an almost insane self-torment and even at the end of the comedy we are not really convinced that he has learned his lesson. One critic thought that his initial 'Distraction and Flutter through the Scene, are fine touches indeed',[43] and another noted that Strictland's difficulty in trusting his servants presented 'so natural and comic a Description of that Disease of the Mind, that the Play, on this Account only, deserves the highest Encomiums.'[44]

The only heavy lines occur in the scenes between Strictland and his wife. As for the rest of the dialogue, we can agree with the opinion given in the *London Chronicle:* 'it is always sensible, often sprightly, and never rises to a Disregard of Nature. Ranger is ever a good Companion, without being a professed Wit; he says lively and spirited Things with an easy and spirited

41 *Catalogue of the Larpent Plays in the Huntington Library* (comp. D. MacMillan, San Marino, California, 1939), p. 11.
42 *The Roman and English Comedy Consider'd* (1747), p. 28.
43 *An Examen of the New Comedy Call'd The Suspicious Husband* (1747), p. 13.
44 *The Roman and English Comedy Consider'd*, p. 27.

PLAYS

Negligence.'⁴⁵ The situations are also well contrived, and the comedy was an outstanding success for many years.

The Jealous Wife was a stock play for even longer, and it has crisp dialogue as well as a nicely calculated plot. Harriot, the heroine, is faced with a wedding to the horse-lover, Sir Harry Beagle, and absconds to the house of her relative, Lady Freelove, who would like to promote the girl's marriage to Lord Trinket. Harriot is in love with Charles Oakly, and he disappoints her by being drunk at an important moment, but reforms and is duly rewarded with her hand. His mother, the jealous wife, is afraid that the girl is adored by her husband (Oakly), but is cured of this and other suspicions by a little rough treatment.

The central situation (III. 2) is cleverly worked up and the resolution follows naturally, even though it turns on Captain O'Cutter's delivering a letter to the wrong person. Since he is a blundering Irishman, this is in character. The others, too, are stock types but Colman manages to give them a certain freshness. The rows between Oakly and his wife are convincing in their association of ideas; Major Oakly is a fire-eater with a sense of humour; Lord Trinket can easily reconcile himself to the ill-success of his intrigues; Sir Harry Beagle gives up his claims on Harriot in some of the most amusing lines of the play: 'It was proposed, you know, to match me with Miss Harriot; but she can't take kindly to me. When one has made a bad bet, it is best to hedge off, you know; and so I have e'en swopped her with Lord Trinket here for his brown horse Nabob, which he bought off Lord Whistle-Jacket, for fifteen hundred guineas.' The broad humour of this statement and the more subtle comedy of other encounters make *The Jealous Wife* a satisfying play.

Colman seems also to have been the main author of *The Clandestine Marriage*, though Garrick was apparently responsible for some initial ideas and scenes as well as a revision of the play. One of the drafts shows him making his notions clear:

⁴⁵ 3–5 February 1757.

Sterling's House   the next morning
Lord Kexsy, at his Toilette, & Levée attending—different Characters of the drama pay their Respects to his Lords[hi]p—here the
whole Character of Kecksy must be pleasantly open'd—his conscious
Superiority over all Mankind in Every thing, his laughing at the
Young Men & Lovewell about their ignorance & Inferiority to
him in Love Matters Knowledge of the Sex, address &c &c &c—to
which *Canton* in Short Speeches plays the back hand of Adulation
& is another Species of the *Bowman* kind; then must enter *Sterling*
who will be a fine Contrast to my Lord with his Vulgar Notions of
Grandeur when Sterling enters—Lord Saplin takes *Lovewell* away
upon some pretence & leaves the Old Gentlemen together—the
finishing of the first Scene of this Act must be left to the fancy of the
Writer—only that after *Sophia* & *Lovewell* are gone out some little
matter of the family Marriage business may be just touch'd upon
that the main stream of the Play may flow through Every Scene of
it, w[hi]ch is not always thought necessary or comply'd with by
our Modern dramatists.[46]

Kexsy was afterwards called Ogleby, and it is likely from
Garrick's description that a parallel with Lord Foppington's
levée in the third scene of *The Relapse* was intended. The great
actor left a strong impression on the comedies that came
before him for perusal and revision. In fact, he later grumbled
that Colman had taunted him with the suggestion that the
Ogleby part of the play 'could only be supported by my own
acting.'[47] The draft is of further interest because so many
comedies of the day were really sets of variations on old themes
with the stage fop, Irishman, sporting squire, heavy father, as
the usual human furniture.

Fortunately *The Clandestine Marriage*, like the other comedies I
have discussed, had far greater life in it than was common in
plays written at the time. Once again the situations are cleverly
selected and the dialogue is spirited. Fanny and Lovewell have
their sentimental moments, but generally the discussions are on
a singularly practical level. This is what may be expected at the

46   II. i. Folger Shakespeare Library MS. Y. d. 114, f.2.
47   *The Letters of David Garrick* (*ed. cit.*), p. 482.

home of Sterling, who is quite willing to allow Sir John Melvil to change his mind about which of Sterling's daughters he will marry, as long as he is also prepared to accept a dowry reduced by twenty thousand pounds. Vulgar wealth gives Sterling and his sister, Mrs. Heidelberg, their claim to be considered the equals of the 'qualaty', represented by the superannuated beau, Lord Ogleby, and his nephew, Sir John. Fanny eventually seeks Ogleby's assistance and he jumps to the conclusion that she is in love with him. When the truth comes out, he still takes her part and persuades her father to pardon her marriage to Lovewell. All this is developed with finesse in a series of amusing scenes, and Sterling and Ogleby linger in the memory as representatives of two sides of mid-eighteenth century civilisation.

The other three plays, *She Stoops to Conquer*, *The Rivals*, and *The School for Scandal*, have been revived so often that their merits are well known, yet perhaps they still need to be placed in their historical context.

In the prologue to *She Stoops to Conquer*, Garrick made laughing reference to tearful comedy and its use of platitudinous sentiments:

> *With a sententious look, that nothing means,*
> *(Faces are blocks, in sentimental scenes)*
> *Thus I begin*—All is not gold that glitters,
> Pleasure seems sweet, but proves a glass of bitters.
> When ign'rance enters, folly is at hand;
> Learning is better far than house and land.
> Let not your virtue trip, who trips may stumble,
> And virtue is not virtue, if she tumble.
>   *I give it up—morals won't do for me;*
> *To make you laugh I must play tragedy.*
> *One hope remains—hearing the maid was ill,*
> A doctor *comes this night to shew his skill.*
> *To cheer her heart, and give your muscles motion,*
> *He in* five draughts *prepar'd, presents a potion.*[48]

[48] Goldsmith, *Collected Works (ed. cit.)*, v. 103.

Dr. Goldsmith demonstrated all his skill in this five-act comedy, and gave the sentimental Comic muse a potion that stopped her crying for some time. He was not interested in moral common-places, preferring to reveal affectionately foibles of character. So Mr. Hardcastle may show a certain sentimentality in his liking for old things, but is otherwise shrewd and level-headed. Tony Lumpkin is a gleeful imp of mischief who grows in authority before our eyes yet is too unsubtle to follow Constance's fibs about the Shakebag club. Marlow, tongue-tied with ladies of fashion, is at ease with a barmaid. Even so minor a personality as the shabby third fellow at the Three Pigeons comes to life in a few lines: 'What, tho' I am obligated to dance a bear, a man may be a gentleman for all that. May this be my poison if my bear ever dances but to the very genteelest of tunes, Water Parted, or the minuet in Ariadne.'

By the side of the men, Kate Hardcastle appears merry-hearted and delightfully sensible, without a touch of oddity or the sentimental in her composition.

The sub-title is *The Mistakes of a Night*, and these are egregious enough to make critics think that the play is really a farce. The dividing line is difficult to place; the mistaking the old mansion for an inn is too long drawn out, and Tony's pretence of driving his mother forty miles to Crackskull Common, as well as her mistaking Hardcastle for a highwayman, are somewhat incredible. Yet Master Tony's fabrications belong to the hearty, rural spirit of the play and are willingly accepted by an audience. Besides, when Hardcastle gives Diggory permission to laugh at the story of the Ould Grouse which they have all laughed at for twenty years, we know we are in the company of a great writer who looked on life, in this play and elsewhere, as the richest of comedies.

Sheridan's *The Rivals* was not a success on its first night, but the author was encouraged by the chief proprietor of Covent Garden Theatre to re-write it: he did so with complete success and the play was produced there in the form we know it, on 28 January 1775. Lydia Languish has a sentimental attitude

M

towards life and wishes it were more like the novels she reads: her desire for a 'conscious moon' and a runaway match in Scotland are amusingly satirised. Sheridan's attitude towards Faulkland is much less direct. Julia knows that her beloved is moody and introspective, but always remembers her gratitude to him for saving her life. His language is that of the sentimental group in *False Delicacy*, stilted and irritating. We tolerate him because he is in love, and that situation is an uncomfortable one, as he himself says: 'O love!—tormentor!—fiend! whose influence, like the moon's, acting on men of dull souls, makes idiots of them, but meeting subtler spirits, betrays their course, and urges sensibility to madness!' He interested and affected audiences in 1775, but is now felt to be rather absurd.

The other characters are much livelier. The scenes between Sir Anthony and Jack Absolute have genius in them. Those in which Jack woos Lydia are highly amusing in their volatility of feeling. Three stock types, Mrs. Malaprop, Acres and Sir Lucius, are vividly, if rather farcically drawn, and give the play a boisterous good humour. The plot is cleverly organised.

So, too, is the structure of *The School for Scandal*. The discussions of scandal are grouped on either side of the main themes concerning the Surfaces and the Teazles, and leading to that piece of virtuosity, the Screen scene. Sheridan's adroitness in making use of material at hand is also to be observed in the casting: every actor was a specialist in the kind of part he was called upon to play, even down to Lamash, who played Trip, the foppish manservant. Whatever their place in society, their lines are witty and telling. Sentiments appear only in an ironical setting, and sentimentality is confined to the tag at the end of the play. *The School for Scandal* was instantly recognised as a great comedy from the school of Congreve, and has never ceased to please.

No scrutiny of the drama in mid-eighteenth century would be complete without a glance at the afterpieces and burlesques that were so popular.

Afterpieces were written to be performed in the later part of a programme, when a full-length tragedy or comedy was over. They were usually restricted to one or two acts, though some of three acts were also given. Quite often they were called farces, but critics thought the name did not accurately describe what some of them offered. The *Universal Museum* (1767) said of Murphy's *The Citizen* that it might be 'called with more propriety than many others, a *comedy*; the principal characters being well drawn from nature, and highly finished; nor is the story and conduct of the piece so very insignificant.' It is certainly full of vitality: the dialogue has a colloquial ring and there is a surprisingly modern note in Quilldrive's phrasing, 'How come you did not leave them at Madam Corinna's?' George Philpot is well drawn: he is a rogue but in his leisure he has a pleasant hobby. He is a 'whip', and the description of his driving is excitingly phrased. Like a typical tradesman, he refuses a challenge to a duel but, and this is quite unusual, he offers to box with his opponent. The rest are types—fox-hunting squire (Sir Jasper), old miser (Old Philpot), and buck (Young Wilding). The action brings them together at the room of Corinna, a harlot. Old Philpot, hiding under the table, hears his son plan to swindle him but betrays his own presence there when his repeater-watch strikes. On the whole, there is sufficient spirit and novelty in the piece to justify the *Universal Museum's* suggested correction.

Twenty years earlier, the nature of farce was mentioned in the prologue to Garrick's afterpiece, *Miss in her Teens* (1747):

> Too long has Farce, neglecting Nature's Laws,
> Debas'd the Stage, and wrong'd the Comic Cause;
> To raise a Laugh has been her sole Pretence
> Tho' clearly purchas'd at the Price of Sense:
> This child of Folly, gain'd Increase with Time;
> Fit for the Place, succeeded *Pantomime*.
> . . . .
> More gen'rous Views inform our Author's Breast,
> From real Life his Characters are drest;
> He seeks to trace the Passions of Mankind,

171

And while he spares the Person, paints the Mind.

Garrick took his theme from D'Ancourt's *La Parisienne*, (1691),[49] but added a fop and turned Angélique into the sixteen-year-old Biddy Bellair, who as a change from her rural pursuits, acts the coquette in London. The most famous episode in the play concerns the duel between Fribble, the fop, and Flash, the braggadocio, in which they continually keep their distance from each other. Puff tries to persuade Fribble that he is hurt, in a paraphrase of Seringe's speech in *The Relapse*: 'Hurt Sir! Why you have—let me see—pray stand in the light—one, two, three through the heart; and let me see—hum—eight through the small guts.' Originality of material was not expected in this genre but liveliness of treatment and a freshness in the dialogue were certainly required. From this point of view, the play was highly successful, and in her romantic notions Biddy has been regarded as a precursor of Lydia Languish. The dialogue is close to real life but the characters belong to the world of fiction.

Foote's two-act farce, *The Author*, may perhaps be considered as an early sample of his work. When it was first performed at Drury Lane on 13 February 1757, the *London Chronicle* remarked: 'There are such strokes of the Bizarre, throughout the Farce, that no body can be present at it without being highly diverted. There is one Scene in which Mr. Foote convinces us that he can copy fron Nature with great Success. The Character of Vamp the Bookseller is drawn with Truth; his Features are acknow-ledged to be exact, without being overcharged in the Colouring. Every Circumstance about Mr. Yates, both in his Dress and Manner, is peculiarly adapted to the Trade; and the Audience are highly pleased with the close imitation of Nature.' The bizarre is always to be found in Foote's work together with personal references that are now difficult to identify. No doubt the 'close imitations of Nature' shown in the portrayal of Vamp allowed many people in the audience to name the

---

[49] On this and other borrowings from the French, see W. A. Kinne, *Revivals and Importations of French Comedies in England, 1749–1800* (New York, 1939), p. 41.

victim, and certain descriptive passages helped them. He was said to boast of his birth yet be full of inconsistencies. 'At the same time that he wou'd take the wall of a Prince of the blood, he wou'd not scruple eating a fryed Sausage, at the Mews Gate.' His function in the play, however, is mainly to make satirical remarks on the bookselling trade. Another fantastic character is Cadwallader, the usual stage Welshman interested only in his pedigree: in it 'there's Welch Princes & Ambassadors, & Kings of Scotland, & Members of Parliament.' Foote's satirical farces are full of such oddities. The dialogue is fast and lively, but the plot is not of much consequence. When he himself became the chief actor in them, they were held together by his remarkable mimicry and topical, scurrilous jests and caricatures. As a contemporary of his said, 'the wit being personal, they depend chiefly upon the acting, and read but indifferently.'[50]

Few of the characters or plots of afterpieces were novel and the audience drew its enjoyment from a rearrangement of well-loved types and situations. The dialogue was usually brisk but not too subtle, and opportunity was given to the actors themselves to improvise business or gags as they wished.

This was particularly true of burlesques, though the period was not really fruitful in them. Sheridan's *The Critic*, the only new one that became popular, was presented nine months after Garrick's death. The vanity of dramatists and the fatuity of the theatrical mania are satirised in the first act. The second contained parodies of some well-known tragic lines. For example, Henry Brook's *Gustavus Vasa* (1739) contains the following:

> Tell him—for once, that I have fought like him,
> And wou'd like him have—
> Conquer'd—he shou'd have said—but there, O there,
> Death sto–pt him short.

Sheridan goes one better:

50 *A Dialogue in the Shades, between the celebrated Mrs. Cibber, and the no less celebrated Mrs. Woffington* (1766), p. 14.

WHISKERANDOS

O cursed parry!—that last thrust in tierce
Was fatal—Captain, thou hast fenced well!
And Whiskerandos quits this bustling scene
For all eter—

BEEFEATER

—nity—He wou'd have added, but stern death
Cut short his being, and the noun at once!

However, *The Critic* mainly laughed at the customary conventions of tragedy. The actors joined in with a will and made fun of each other and of personalities of the day. As time went on, they added new lines and omitted others. They also took great care to see that the topical references were brought up to date.

The best entertainments of the period, then, were comic in tone and often satirical in intention. New tragedies were very rarely successful, and their place was usurped by sentimental comedy that substituted pity for terror and left the audience in a state of heartfelt woe.

Garrick as Macbeth.

CHAPTER NINE

Theatres outside London

The Licensing Act of 1737 confined acting in London to the patent theatres and forbade performances in the rest of the country:

> ... from and after the twenty-fourth of *June*, one thousand seven hundred and thirty seven, every Person who shall for Hire, Gain, or Reward, act, represent, or perform, any Interlude, Tragedy, Comedy, Opera, Play, Farce, or other Entertainment of the Stage, or any Part or Parts therein, in case such Person shall not have any legal Settlement in the Place where the same shall be acted, represented, or performed, without Authority by virtue of Letters Patent from his Majesty, his Heirs, Sucessors, or Predecessors, or without licence from the Lord Chamberlain of his Majesty's Household for the time being, shall be deemed to be a Rogue and a Vagabond within the Intent and Meaning of the said recited Act, and shall be liable and subject to all such Penalties and Punishments. . . .

Knowing the terms of the act, the manager of a travelling company sought from a mayor or magistrate not permission to perform but mere goodwill. Old soldiers and sailors often met with cordiality. Freemasons received encouragement from a brother. The rest had to earn toleration by proving that they were respectable and by giving at least one performance in aid of a charity. They could also be useful in a neighbourhood by supplying local needs: for example, Whitlock of the Chester company acted as 'an operator of the teeth.' Others painted inn signs or gave music lessons.

Since 'Jacks in office' were frequently changeable and arbitrary, the actors advertised their performances in words that usually allowed them to evade the terms of the act. Only a year before she made her first London appearance, Sarah Siddons was a member of a troupe that used this method of preserving their livelihood. Their notice ran: 'By the Wolverhampton Company of Comedians (at the Theatre) this present Monday July 11 [1774] a Concert of Vocal and Instrumental music; between the Several Parts of the Concert will be played (Gratis) the celebrated Comedy The West Indian. ... N.B. There will be no Gold taken at the Door.'[1] People who attended paid only for the concert, and saw the rehearsal of the play free. The equivocation served its purpose often enough, but was of little use if the magistrates wanted to shut up an entertainment. The truth of this can be proved from a case at Bristol in 1773: 'By Virtue of an Information lodged against the Performers at the Theatrical Concert at the Coopers Hall, they were summoned and attended at the Council House on Wednesday, and the Magistrates, after hearing arguments on both sides, levied a fine of £50 on each of the four performers, for acting some part or parts of plays.'[2]

No town outside London could supply audiences large enough to support actors for long, so their seasons usually lasted for three months or less, according to the warmth of the welcome they received. Then they moved elsewhere, and repeated their repertoire. The poorest of them walked from town to town, following the wagons that carried their scenery and properties. The better-off looked down on them as 'banditti' or 'scalping parties', fit only for barns. They were the subject of many a derisory jest, like the one told of Kearns, a stroller who was brought before the magistrate and asked his profession:

---

1 *Aris's Birmingham Gazette*, 18 July 1774. Bad gold coins were not uncommon.

2 *Daily Advertiser*, 26 January 1773.

'I plays all the tyrants in tragedy.'
'And what do you get by that, friend?'
'Seven shillings a week, your honour, and finds my own jewels.'[3]

Yet many an actor began his career in these small troupes, before joining a better company playing regularly in a number of county towns. They were often made up of a family group with some additions drawn either from other well-known acting families or, less frequently, from those who had no actors in their genealogical tree. Whatever their background, it was essential that they should contribute to the reputation for respectability that a company enjoyed. This is very evident in the following advertisement for recruits:

TO THEATRICAL GENIUS

Wanted, for a reputable Company of Comedians, several ACTORS and ACTRESSES, of character and address, who can make a genteel appearance in life. The greater encouragement will be given to persons of merit, and the preference to those who are well studied. The Company's constant receipts admit of a livelihood superior to most that travel, and is conducted with as much regularity and decorum as a Theatre-Royal.

Any Lady or Gentleman, possessed of a good figure and talents for the stage, shall have a fair trial, a candid decision of their abilities, and every assistance to enable them to cut a figure in that profession. The present Proprietor and Manager would have no objection to entering into a partnership with any Lady or Gentleman, that could command an equal capital with himself. Whoever may be inclined to treat on that head, must have for £100 to £200 at their own disposal, which circumstance is mentioned to prevent unnecessary trouble.

N.B. As a number of applications are expected, many perhaps (from old Strolers) out of curiosity, no letters but what are Post paid will be given the least attention to, or received; and, to prevent any impositions no money will be advanced to any Performer, 'till they arrive on the spot, nor any travelling charges allowed 'till the expiration of one year from the day of joining the Company.

Letters addressed (post-paid) to Capt. Roger Knight, at Cannon's

3 *The Theatrical Jester* (n.d.), p. 9.   177

Ball, in the borough of Minehead, Somersetshire will be immediately answered.

Reputation was a jewel managers flashed before everyone's eyes, as they made up circuits of towns they could visit year after year. Wherever the gentry gathered, the players were in attendance upon them. Performances were given at one town during the Quarter Sessions; at another, during the race meeting or the Michaelmas fair. When sea-bathing became an elegant indulgence, the actors dispelled tedium by entertaining the visitors to the resorts during the evening. Their willingness to place themselves unreservedly at the disposal of their patrons is plain in an advertisement of the Brighton theatre in 1770: 'Mr. Johnson proposes to perform the celebrated Mr. Foote's comedies once a week in the day-time, to begin precisely at one o'clock and conclude half-an-hour after two. Any morning so wet as to prevent the gentry riding out, they will begin at twelve and furnish proper amusement till two.'[4]

Few English towns of any size escaped a visit by the players. For example, Worcester was gratified in 1768 by the following notice: 'Mr. Kemble begs Leave to inform the Ladies and Gentlemen that the Theatre at the King's Head is compleatly fitted up, and constant Fires have been kept this Fortnight past, to air the House, which will open on Saturday next; and the Publick may depend that the Company will exert their utmost Abilities to entertain the Audience in a most agreeable Manner, through a grateful Remembrance of the many Favours they have already received from the worthy Inhabitants of this City and its Neighbourhood.'[5] Of Uttoxeter in 1772, it was reported: 'There is a new and commodious Theatre erected in the Cockpit at the Sign of the Black Swan, where there will be a regular Play and Entertainment performed every Monday, Wednesday, and Friday, from this present Time till the Middle

---

4 H. C. Porter, *The History of the Theatres of Brighton from 1774 to 1885* (Brighton, 1886), p. 3.

5 *Berrow's Worcester Journal*, 24 November 1768.

of July next, by Mr. Carleton's Company of Comedians,'[6] The
two companies were unfortunate enough to clash at Coventry
in the summer of 1773, when Carleton opened his 'New Concert
Room' in the Half Moon Yard, and Kemble's people played at
the Draper's Hall.[7] Competition everywhere was so severe that
She Stoops to Conquer was acted by Stanton's company at Tam-
worth Town Hall within a month of the play's first performance
at Covent Garden.

Some managers looked for audiences in garrison towns or
seaports. Mrs. Baker took her troupe between 1772 and 1777
to Dover, Rochester, Faversham, Folkestone, Deal and
Sandwich.[8] The players at Winchester and Salisbury found
good support at Portsmouth from sailors. Seamen were also a
useful part of the audience at North Shields, and the poet John
Cunningham wrote a prologue, supposed to be spoken by a
sailor there:

> [*Without*] Hollo! my masters, where d'ye mean to stow us?
> We're come to see what pastime ye can shew us;
> SAL, step aloft, you shan't be long without me,
> I'll walk their quarter-deck and look about me. [*Enters*]
> Tom and Dick Topsail are above—I hear 'em,
> Tell 'em to keep a berth, and Sal—sit near 'em:
> Sal's a smart lass: I'd hold a butt of stingo
> In three weeks' time she'd learn the playhouse lingo:
> She loves your plays, she understands their meaning;
> She calls 'em—MORAL RULES made entertaining.
> Your Shakespeare books, she knows 'em to a tittle,
> And I myself (at sea) have read—a little.
>   At London, Sirs, when Sal and I were courting,
> I tow'd her ev'ry night a playhouse sporting.
> Mass! I could like 'em and their whole 'Paratus,
> But for their fidlers and their damn'd Sonatas.—
> Give me the merry sons of guts and rosin,

6 *Aris's Birmingham Gazette*, 18 May 1772.
7 *Jopson's Coventry Mercury*, 12 and 19 July, 13 September 1773.
8 Norma Hodgson, 'Sarah Baker, 1736/7–1816', *Studies in English
Theatre History* (1952), p. 67.

That play—God save the King, and Nancy Dawson.

[*Looking about*]

Well—tho' the frigates' not so much bedoyzen'd,

'Tis snug enough—'Tis clever for the size on't!

. . . . 9

Other managers found audiences wherever they could and by covering great distances. James Whitley's circuit, between 1750 and 1780, took in visits to Leeds, Stamford, Chester, Manchester, Preston, Lancaster, Nottingham, Derby and Worcester, with forays into East Anglia.[10] Joseph Austin and his partners acted at Shrewsbury, Bridgnorth, Wrexham, Chester, Newcastle and Lancaster. 'This', said Austin in one of his appeals, 'is the Aera of the theatrical Age, and . . . theatrical Amusements are not only generally thought the most rational Way of passing a few Hours of a Winter Evening but are honoured with the Patronage and frequent Presence of the GREATEST PERSONAGE in this Kingdom.' He added that 'drawing Gentlemen and Ladies into the town [Newcastle] . . . will be beneficial to the lower Class of trading People in general.'[11] These were the usual themes of an appeal for support.

Opposition was based on different reasons. Godly people had always feared the playhouse because it was a worldy entertainment and its chief attractions were actresses. Their morals were often little better than those of the whores in the galleries. Besides, attendance at the theatre was a waste of precious time. This might be pardoned in the wealthy who had so little to do, but could not be forgiven in the lower classes when they forsook their duties for vain amusements. The double force of the attack is to be seen in the denunciation of playhouses by the Edinburgh and Glasgow presbyteries in 1757: 'Such Entertainments, from what has usually been exhibited in them, and also from the dissolute Lives (for the most part) and infamous characters

9 *London Chronicle*, 12–15 October 1765.

10 J. L. Hodgkinson and Rex Pogson, *The Early Manchester Theatre* (1960), pp. 25–31, 43–68.

11 C. Price, 'Joseph Austin and his Associates, 1766–1789, '*Theatre Notebook*, iv (1950), 89–94.

of the Players, have been looked upon by the Christian Church of all Ages, and of all different Communions, as extremely prejudicial to Religion and Morality, as well as hurtful to the other valuable Interests of human Society, by the wasteful Expence of Money and Time they have occasioned.' The last clause was amplified in a further statement: 'To enumerate how many Servants, Apprentices, and Students in different Branches of Literature, in this City [Edinburgh] and Suburbs, have been seduced from their proper Business, by attending the Stage, would be a painful and disagreeable Task.'[12] The players were doubly culpable: in their daily lives they were dissolute, and in their vocations they disturbed settled communities by taking people's minds from their work and artfully suggesting the more pleasurable world of the imagination.

Yet the indignation of the religious opponents of the theatre did little to stop the growing delight in plays, and the actors who had once been satisfied to perform in town halls or the great rooms of inns were soon accommodated in specially built theatres. Their increased influence and social prestige can best be seen in the fact that seven provincial theatres were given royal patents between 1768 and 1779.

In many ways the most interesting—if not the most typical— is Bath. Before the middle of the century, performances were given at Lady Hawley's assembly rooms,[13] in a large room at the George and another at the Globe, as well as in the 'New Theatre' (fifty feet by twenty-five) in Kingsmead Street.[14] The generally unsatisfactory nature of the accommodation is noted in proposals made by John Hippisley, manager of Jacob's Well Theatre, Bristol, and printed in the *Bath Journal*, 7 December 1747:

Theatrical Performances, when conducted with Decency and Regu-

12 *London Chronicle*, 19–22 February, 8–10 March 1757.
13 Her death is reported in the *Bath Journal*, 4 February 1744–5. See, also, Sybil Rosenfeld, *Strolling Players and Drama in the Provinces, 1660–1765* (Cambridge, 1939), p. 178.
14 B. S. Penley, *The Bath Stage* (1892), pp. 21–2; *Bath Journal*, 22 February 1748.

larity, have been always esteem'd the most rational Amusements, by the Polite and Thinking Part of Mankind:- Strangers, therefore, must be greatly surpriz'd to find, at BATH, Entertainments of this Sort in no better Perfection than they are; and it is a Place, during its Seasons, honour'd with so great a number of Persons, eminent for *Politeness, Judgment* and *Taste*; and where might be reasonably expected (next to London) the best Theatre in England.

The present *Play-House*, or rather *Play-Room*, is so small and incommodious, that 'tis almost impossible to have things better done in it than they are. The Profits arising from the Performance, as now conducted, will not support a larger, or better, Company of Actors: And nothing can be more disagreeable, than for Persons of the first *Quality*, and those of the *lowest Rank* to be seated on the same Bench together. . . .

Hippisley went on to suggest that a new playhouse be built, but died shortly afterwards, and his project was taken up by a local brewer, John Palmer. He sought subscribers at fifty pounds a share, and offered in return one shilling a night for seventy nights and a silver ticket for free admission. The new playhouse was opened in Orchard Street in 1750, and was to be the main theatrical centre in Bath for the rest of the century. Until 1753, it had to share the favours of the nobility with Brown's company playing at Simpson's (earlier Lady Hawley's) rooms. For example, in 1752 *Merope* was bespoken at Simpson's by Lady Betty Bathurst and *The Merry Wives of Windsor* by the Countess of Northumberland, while Lady Throckmorton asked for *The Beggar's Opera* at Orchard Street, and Viscountess Torrington *The Orphan*.[15] Neither house could make an adequate living so Simpson was paid two hundred pounds a year to shut his, and Palmer bought out the other subscribers to Orchard Street and dominated the situation at Bath.[16] With the aid of his son, he was able to apply to parliament for a patent for his theatre, and the hope of a new status stirred up controversy at the spa. Eleven articles by 'Frank Freeman' appeared in the

15 *Bath Journal*, 20 January, 10 February, 16 March, 18 May 1752.
16 *The Life and Adventures of Timothy Ginnadrake* (1771), iii. 35.

Bath Chronicle between 8 October and 17 December 1767 that criticised the company playing at Orchard Street rather heavily. Nevertheless the patent was duly granted in 1768 and the Bath Theatre became the most important one outside London. John Henderson and Sarah Siddons left its boards for instant fame at Drury Lane Theatre.

Bristol had far more difficulty than Bath in gaining royal approval for its theatre. It was a great trading centre and had a large population. It could also boast a spa for fashionable visitors at Clifton Wells, yet the opposition to the playhouse by commercial interests and religious people remained strong throughout the period. As early as October 1704, the actors were presented at the Quarter Sessions on the ground that plays were 'attended with all manner of profaneness, lewdness, murthers' and that they 'debauch our Youth and utterly ruin many Apprentices and Servants, already so Unruly and Licentious.'[17] Much the same point of view was put forward in the year 1778, when application was made for a patent. A letter to 'the Trading and Religious Part of the Citizens of Bristol' read: 'I fear you do not see in a proper light the great danger of having a play house licensed in this city. A Bill for that purpose is now before the House. If that it should pass, the probable consequence will be that we shall have performances in the winter. How that may affect the morals of our sons, daughters and apprentices and servants when they can conceal themselves by the darkness of the night is but too apparent.' The writer went on to call for a public meeting 'to stem the torrent of vice.'[18] In spite of these hostile forces, the bill was passed and the Lord Chamberlain was empowered, in the same year, to license the theatre there.

The bill probably won support because these theatres had been properly conducted over the previous fifty years. Between

---

17 See the presentment printed by G. T. Watts, *Theatrical Bristol* (Bristol, 1915), p. 21.
18 Richard Smith's MSS. on the Bristol Theatre (in Bristol Public Library), volume for 1766–1841.

1729 and 1765 the playhouse at Jacob's Well became the Bristol centre for a company from the London theatres. It played there in June, July and August, when the metropolitan houses were closed, and was managed by John Hippisley, creator of Peachum in *The Beggar's Opera* and author of a farce called *A Journey to Bristol, or, the Honest Welchman* (1731). Jacob's Well lay outside the city but was 'convenient for Coaches as well as for the Rope Walk leading to the Hot-Well.'[19] Its company was a sharing one, the takings being divided equally between the players, once expenses had been met and allowance made for scenery and costumes. Each member took £8 14s. od. for the 1741 season, but the sum had increased to £27 7s. od. by 1748, a sure proof of the growing popularity of these performers. Among them were Macklin, Woodward, and Mrs. Pritchard.[20]

Hippisley died on 12 February 1748, and a piece of doggerel summed up his progress from candle-snuffer for the Bath company and the collier in Farquhar's *The Recruiting Officer* to well-liked manager:

Here lies John Hip'sley, dead in Truth,—
Who oft, in *Jest*, dy'd in his Youth;
Prefer'd from Candle-Snuffing Art,
He with Applause play'd many a Part.
The *Collier* first advanc'd him higher;
Next Gomez plagu'd with Wife and Fryar:
Fam'd in *Fluellin, Pistol's* Hector;
Then was of Play-Houses Projector;
An Author too, and wrote a Farce;
And there, all say, he shew'd his A--e.
If acting well a Soul will save,
His sure a Place in Heav'n shall have:
And yet, to speak the Truth, I ween,
As great a SCRUB as e'er was seen.[21]

19 *London Weekly Advertiser*, 28 June 1729, quoted by G. T. Watts, p. 41.
20 Sybil Rosenfeld, 'Actors in Bristol, 1741–1748', *The Times Literary Supplement*, 29 August 1936, p. 700.
21 *Bath Journal*, 22 February 1747/8. The allusion to Scrub is to the simple but cunning servant in Farquhar's *The Beaux Stratagem*.

Jacob's Well continued to attract good audiences for many summers but, in 1764-5, a new playhouse was built in King Street. In spite of the usual opposition, a sum of five thousand pounds was subscribed and the theatre opened on 30 May 1766. Its appeal to the various classes may be assessed from the accommodation provided: the boxes held 750 people, the pit, 320, and the gallery, 530.[22]

The two actors, who gave Bristol most delight in the sixties (at Jacob's Well as much as King Street), were William Powell and Charles Holland. The stage career of Powell was brief, extending over only six years. In that time he moved from the position of leading actor while Garrick was on the continent, to that of a rival who could challenge his master in some of his parts. He was an actor who lived by inspiration rather than discipline, and Chatterton wrote some eulogistic lines on him:

> Where oft our Powell, Nature's genuine son,
> With tragic tones the fix'd attention won:
> Fierce from his lips his angry accents fly,
> Fierce as the blast that tears the northern sky;
> Like snows that trickle down hot Aetna's steep,
> His passion melts the soul and makes us weep:
> But O! how soft his tender accents move—
> Soft as the cooings of the turtle's love—
> Soft as the breath of morn in bloom of spring
> Dropping a lucid tear on Zephyr's wing:
> O'er Shakespeare's varied scenes he wander'd wide,
> In Macbeth's form all human pow'r defy'd;
> In shapeless Richard's dark and fierce disguise,
> In dreams he saw the murder'd train arise;
> Then what convulsions shook his trembling breast,
> And strew'd with pointed thorns his bed of rest!
> But fate has snatch'd thee—early was thy doom,
> How soon enclos'd within the silent tomb!
> . . . .

[22] Richard Jenkins, *Memoirs of the Bristol Stage* (Bristol, 1826), pp. 66–9, 74.

N

> Without thy pow'rful aid, the languid stage
> No more can please at once and mend the age.[23]

Chatterton also admired Holland's mastery of tragic effect, his majesty, terror, pity. The poet's awe was summed up in his line, 'But nature on thy soul has stamp'd the God.'[24] Both Powell and Holland died in 1769, the one at thirty-four and the other at thirty-six. Their loss was keenly felt in Bristol and in London.

When the King Street Theatre was eventually granted a licence by the Lord Chamberlain, its letters patent contained some sentences that are worth noting. Plays containing 'any passages or Expressions Offensive to piety and good Manners' or material 'whereby the Christian Religion in General or the Church of England may in any manner Suffer Reproach', were not to be produced. The licensee was also directed to exercise 'the Strictest Regard to such Representations as any way Concern Civil polity or the Constitution of our Government that those may Contribute to the Support of our Sacred Authority and the preservation of Order.' The purpose of the theatre was epitomised as 'honest recreation.'[25]

In many ways the history of the Birmingham theatre resembles that of Bristol. In the summer months it was visited by a London company that met with much opposition from the religious and trading interests. A theatre of sorts was arranged in the early forties in a yard off Moor Street, and there Richard Yates and his fellows put on regular performances. Their building was sufficiently sophisticated for them to advertise that 'No person can be admitted behind the scenes, on account of the Machinery.'[26]

The analogy with Bristol even extended to the siting in King

23 T. Chatterton, *The Complete Works* (ed. D. S. Taylor, Oxford, 1971), i. 344.
24 *Ibid.*, i. 340.
25 The Letters Patent are quoted in full by G. T. Watts, *op. cit.*, pp. 124–8.
26 Quoted from *Aris's Birmingham Gazette*, by J. E. Cunningham, *Theatre Royal* (Oxford, 1950), p. 12.

Street of the new theatre built for Yates and opened in 1752. The population grew and interest in plays increased so much that another theatre for Yates was ready in 1774 and, three years later, he applied to parliament for permission to act there. At this point the analogy with Bristol breaks down: a licence was not granted. The question was discussed fiercely in the House of Commons, when one member had stated that he disliked licensed theatres in manufacturing towns. He added that theatre tickets had been forced on work people in place of wages, and that in their poverty young women had turned to prostitution. Charles James Fox argued, however, that theatres had been encouraged by the magistrates in Birmingham for many years and that many people must be thought to favour them: 'In his opinion, dramatic exhibitions had their use everywhere, and often drew the attention of the common people, and prevented them from wasting their time and money in employment of a much more dangerous and pernicious nature.'[27] Opposition prevailed, and Birmingham Theatre did not obtain a licence from the Lord Chamberlain for another thirty years. This was quite unusual, for the other large towns were given letters patent if they had local support.

For example, Norwich was the leading inland town of the Kingdom and was noted for its manufacture of 'crapes, bombazines, and other stuffs'.[28] From 1731 to 1757, performances by the Norwich Company of Comedians were given at a playhouse at the White Swan, but the local gentlemen who had subscribed to the erection of elegant assembly rooms felt that a more suitable theatre was also required and encouraged Thomas Ivory to build one. It was opened in 1758, and the Norwich company was engaged to perform there. Ten years later, an act of parliament giving the Lord Chamberlain authority to license it was passed and Ivory sold out to subscribers. They proceeded to keep minute books of the committee of management, and these reveal a strong effort to emulate London, in

27 *The Parliamentary History of England* (1814), xix. 198–200.
28 R. Brookes, *The General Gazetteer* (10th ed., 1797).

careful regulations preventing people (even if belonging to the committee of management) from going behind the scenes. They also sent the manager himself to Drury Lane to see Garrick's *A Christmas Tale* so that it might reach the highest standards when presented locally.[29]

Norwich was different from Bristol and Birmingham in that it was not visited by a company of London players, but was the centre for a troupe that also played at other towns in East Anglia. Thomas Ivory had built for it another theatre at Colchester, and seasons were also given at Yarmouth, Bury St. Edmunds and Bungay. In fact, the Norwich company depended for its prosperity on the support it could muster in these towns, and the committee of management of the Norwich Theatre grew so alarmed at the competition from other players that it thought of bringing a bill into parliament to try to limit performances in those places to its company alone.[30]

At Liverpool, a licence from the Lord Chamberlain was secured with some difficulty, though plays had long been given for summer visitors to this seaside resort. Irish companies had acted there in the early forties. By 1756, a traveller could mention that Liverpool had its own 'Musick-Meetings, Assemblies, etc., and a neat theatre that maintains a set of comedians for four months in the year very well.'[31] These seasons at the Liverpool Drury Lane Theatre were the prerogative of the London players, under Gibson of Covent Garden, and they acted each Monday, Wednesday, and Friday. On 6 August 1756, Ned Shuter sang 'The Dust Cart',[32] an amusing 'cantata' from the Haymarket performances of Christopher Smart's *Old Woman's Oratory*:

> As Tink'ring Tom the Streets his trade did cry,
> He saw his lovely Silvia passing by,

29 *The Committee Books of the Theatre Royal, Norwich, 1768–1825* (ed. Dorothy H. Eshleman, 1970), pp. 15–18, 24, 48.
30 *Ibid.*, p. 46.
31 Quoted in R. J. Broadbent, *Annals of the Liverpool Stage* (Liverpool, 1908), p. 19.
32 *Ibid.*, p. 29.

In Dust Cart high advanced the Nymph was plac'd
With the rich Cinders round her lovely Waist.
Tom with uplifted Hands th'occasion blest
And thus in soothing Strains the Maid addrest:
   'Oh *Silvia*! while you drive your Carts
   To pick up Dust you steal our Hearts.
   You take our Dust and steal our Hearts.
   That mine is gone, alas! tis true,
   And dwells among the Dust—with you.
   O lovely *Silvia*, ease my pain!
   Give me the Heart you stole, again.'
Silvia advanc'd above the Rabble rout,
Exulting roll'd her sparkling Eyes about.
She heav'd her swelling Breast as black as sloe
And look'd disdain on little Folks below:
To Tom she nodded as the Carr drew on
And then resolv'd to speak she cried, 'Stop, John!
   Shall I who ride above the rest
   Be by a paltry Crowd opprest,
   Ambition now my Soul does fire,
   The Youths shall languish and admire:
   And ev'ry Girl with anxious Heart,
   Shall long to ride in my Dust Cart.'

Shuter's monologues and songs were to be part of the staple entertainment at Liverpool for many years, with dances by Mr. and Mrs. Granier as well as a play and a farce. Samuel Derrick, soon to become Master of Ceremonies at Bath, visited the theatre in 1760, found the scenery pretty, and the costumes rich. He also mentioned that 'behind the boxes there is a table spread, in the manner of a coffee-house, with tea, coffee, wines, cakes, fruit and punch, where a woman attends to accommodate the company on very moderate terms.'[33]

William Gibson made sure that the company enjoyed a sound reputation by paying all bills promptly, and was so esteemed that he felt able to appeal to the Corporation for help in getting a royal licence for a new theatre. The Corporation

33 Derrick, *Letters written from Leverpoole* (1767), i. 20.

decided on 7 December 1768 not to give a further licence to the playhouse that was in being, because it was 'in a very dangerous place for company to resort to on account of the narrow streets'; but to support Gibson's petition and pray that the Lord Chamberlain 'grant the same licence and no other, as was granted to Norwich, and all proceedings be done at Mr. Gibson's expense.'[34]

The first petition was passed by the Commons but not by the Lords. At the second attempt (January 1771), the bill was accepted and, in April, Gibson was given a patent for twenty-one years to establish a theatre in Liverpool and keep a company there 'for his Majesty's service.'[35] The new playhouse was opened in June, but Gibson himself died in August.

A couple of accounts belonging to the Theatre for the years 1776–8 are still extant, and take us right into its daily running. Look at the following payments:

1776 June 8   By Lockwood's Bill for getting the Scenes ready—a man cleaning them with Bread

2 weeks carr[y]ing out Play Bills &c.	£1. 6. o.
July 15 By a Book of Catherine & Petruchio and one of Jealous Wife	2. 6
July 26 By Cash to Bell Man for warning the Pantomime's not being done	1. o.
Aug 31 By a Labourer for Carry[y]ing out Rubbish from the Cellar from New Traps	3. o.
Sept 3 By Hall for writing Parts	2. 2½
Sept 14 By Mr. Smith for writing Soft Music for Maid of the Oaks	5. o
Sept 16 By Mr. DuBellamy for a Score of the Deserter lost	6. o
Sept 16 By Bolton for repairing the Harps[ichor]d	5. o
By Charles Pickering for taking care of the Theatre 1775 and Meal for the Dog	2. 9. 6

The list of salaries is also given, and shows that Mrs. Siddons

34 R. J. Broadbent, *op. cit.*, p. 44, quoting from the Corporation Records.
35 *Ibid.*, p. 48.

received as much as the best male actor—£1 11s. 6d. a week. Miss Farren and Mrs. Inchbald, who were also to become famous, received the same.[36]

Their names remind us that the Liverpool troupe was not now composed only of London players, but had become a stock company supplemented during the summer by comparatively few metropolitan performers. In the rest of the year it sought audiences at Manchester and elsewhere, just as the Bristol company linked itself, at this period, to Bath.

In the middle of the eighteenth century, Manchester was a country town of not quite twenty-thousand inhabitants. By 1779 it was growing rapidly but was not yet a leading industrial centre. With the increase of population came greater encouragement for the players. Whitley brought his company to the 'New Theatre, the Upper end of King Street' in 1760 and 1761, and ended his seasons in style by making handsome donations of fifty pounds and thirty-one pounds to the Manchester Infirmary. Between 1762 and 1765, summer seasons were given by London companies under, first, Ross, then, Lee. Whitley put on winter seasons again between 1766 and 1775.[37]

Application to parliament for a licence to perform at the theatre being built at Manchester, was made in 1775 by two Covent Garden actors, Joseph Younger and George Mattocks. The subject was debated at length in the House of Lords. The Bishop of London was of the opinion that theatres should be confined to the capital: 'there under the most cultivated eyes the stage is the least pernicious.' He was strongly opposed by the Earl of Carlisle, who declared that 'manufactory towns have of late been the particular receptacles of methodism; I know not of any way so effectual to eradicate that dark, odious and ridiculous enthusiasm, as by giving to the people chearful, rational amusements, which may operate against their methodistical melancholy.'[38]

---

[36] Folger Shakespeare Library MS. Z. e. 20.
[37] J. L. Hodgkinson and Rex Pogson, *The Early Manchester Theatre* (1960), pp. 25–59.　　　[38] *London Chronicle*, 13–16 May 1775.

Approval was duly given, and letters patent were granted in July 1775. The new playhouse was 'a plain brick building . . . 102 feet long and 48 feet broad,'[39] and it was soon to accommodate perhaps the most talented company of young people ever to grace the provincial stage. After a summer season at Birmingham and an autumn at Liverpool, Younger and Mattocks brought their players to Manchester for a programme that lasted from December 1776 to 21 March 1777. Mrs. Siddons performed, among others, the parts of Desdemona, Lady Randolph, Portia, Angelica (*Love for Love*), Cleopatra (*All for Love*), Indiana, and Hamlet. She delivered Sheridan's epilogue to *Semiramis* 'exceedingly well', and on her benefit night, recited her own composition, 'A Poetical Address to the Town of Manchester.'[40] Among the other players were her brother, John Philip Kemble, as well as Miss Farren and Mrs. Inchbald. The company seems to have been able to provide spectacular scenes as well as fine acting, and in *Cymon* there were to be seen a flying chariot drawn by eagles, a transparent cave of Merlin, and a view of a burning lake.[41]

Mrs. Siddons and her husband left Manchester to play at York for a short period. The city had a long connection with actors, and in the early eighteenth century subscribers had paid fifteen shillings a head to persuade players to entertain them twice a week during the winter.[42] The theatre was granted letters patent in 1769, and Tate Wilkinson took over its direction. In 1795, he published *The Wandering Patentee*, that described his experiences on his circuit of theatres[43] and made plain the delight with which he recalled his situation at York in the seventies: 'I was high in public favour, and do not remember any season from that period to this when the theatre was so

39 J. L. Hodgkinson and R. Pogson, *op. cit.*, p. 11, quoting Aston's *Manchester Guide* (1804).
40 *Manchester Mercury*, 20–27 January, 4, 18 February, 18 March 1777.
41 *Ibid.*, 27 January 1777.
42 M. H. Dodds, 'The Northern Stage', *Archeologia Aeliana*, 3rd ser., xi (1914), 53–4.
43 Hull was also granted letters patent in 1769.

regularly and fashionably attended: There was a remarkable number of genteel families that year at York, which must ever preponderate in favour of a Theatre, provided they are theatrically inclined, which is not always the case. I do not recollect so numerous a resort of leading families since that year [1771].'[44] Mrs. Siddons certainly had a good reception there in the spring of 1777, playing Matilda as well as Lady Alton, and repeating the parts of Indiana and Semiramis that she had played at Manchester. At the benefit performance she shared with her husband on 17 May, she played the 'breeches' role of Sir Harry Wildair, and other attractions included Tate Wilkinson as Lady Pentweazle in Foote's *Diversions of the Morning* as well as a 'pantomimical interlude call'd *The Masquerade*, when the stage will be illuminated with upwards of five hundred lights.'[45]

All these provincial theatres were accustomed to performing the London repertoire of old plays, and of putting on new attractions from Covent Garden or Drury Lane as soon as they could do so. Sometimes they were given permission to act a new success as a favour or at a fee 'for one night only'; occasionally they obtained a text by surreptitious means.

They were now able to demonstrate their growing strength by presenting original plays for the first time. The most important of these was *Douglas*, given at Edinburgh, and while there is nothing of comparable interest in the rest of the period, some titles are worth noting because they reveal creative activity outside London. At Bristol, William Combe's farce, *The Flattering Milliner* was performed at the King Street Theatre for Henderson's benefit on 11 September 1775. Combe was later to make a name for himself as the creator of Dr. Syntax.[46] At Richmond, Edward Thompson's *St. Helena* was given in 1776. At Manchester, John Philip Kemble's farce, *The Female Officer*, was acted in 1778, and the same player's

44 (York, 1795), i. 81.
45 *York Courant*, 15, 22, 29 April, 6, 13 May 1777.
46 H. W. Hamilton, *Dr. Syntax* (1969), pp. 48–52.

interlude, *The School for Scandal Scandaliz'd*, was put on at York in March 1779. In fact, several other new pieces were presented at Tate Wilkinson's theatres in York and Hull, and some of them were also published. They include two five-act comedies by Robert Hitchcock, another (*The Mercantile Lovers*) by George Wallis, and a farce, *The Volunteers*, probably by William Woods.[47]

The provincial theatres achieved their new status through the support of influential people. Naturally, then, they were also used whenever possible as meeting places of the well-to-do, even when they were not open as playhouses. For the purpose of assembly or dancing, the pit was covered over with an extra floor, as may be noted in the advertisement of another theatre licensed in this period. When the 'Theatre Royal on Richmond Green' came up for sale in London in August 1776, there was among the items 'a compleat framed door to cover the stage and pitt for occasionally converting it into an Assembly Room with all proper materials for that purpose.'[48]

The more the theatre became a valued amenity in a town, the more prosperous grew the players. Once they had a secure base, they could establish new playhouses elsewhere and add to their circuits. So they became quite respectable members of local society, even admired sometimes for their command of Shakespeare and knowledge of the arts.

Their old reputations as shiftless and untrustworthy fitted only the poorest members of the profession. Fortune did not favour those who acted in small towns and villages: their lot was as hard as ever. Some inkling of it is to be found in the lines of a prologue, written by the Rev. Joseph Hazard[49] and spoken by a member of a company of strollers in a barn in the West of England:

47 *Catalogue of the Larpent Plays in the Huntington Library* (comp. D. Mac-Millan, San Marino, 1939), pp. 59, 68, 71, 75, 77, 80. Kemble also wrote a five-act tragedy, *Belisarius*.
48 *Morning Chronicle*, 19 August 1776.
49 Add. MS. 5843.

Hard is the Fortune of a strolling Play'r!
Necessity's rough Burden doom'd to bear:
And scanty is the Pittance he can earn,
Wand'ring from Town to Town, from Barn to Barn.
This might content us but the Contrast great
Adds to the Terror of our changeful Fate.
He who to Night is seated on his Throne
Calls Subjects, Kingdoms, Empires, all his own.
Who wears the Diadem & Regal Robe
Next Morning shall awake—As poor as Job.
'Where are my forty Knights?' cries frantic Lear.
A Page replies,—'Your Majesty, they're here.'
When lo!—Two Bailiffs & a Writ appear.
'Give me a Pound of Flesh,' cries Shylock, well he may
For Shylock—has not eat an Ounce to Day.

Some of them escaped from their tribulations after a short time and joined better companies, then progressed to the Theatres Royal, and were eventually recommended by some influential patron to the managers of Covent Garden or Drury Lane. Others made fortunate marriages: Thomas Snagg eloped with Elizabeth Garstin[50] and came into a considerable estate, and Joseph Austin took a bride of 'near ninety' with fourteen thousand pounds.[51] For the majority, a strolling existence was all they were to know and their only appearances in London were at the booths of Bartholomew Fair.[52]

50 T. Snagg, *Recollections of Occurrences* (1951), p. xviii.
51 *Westminster Journal*, 28 September 1771.
52 For which, see Sybil Rosenfeld, *The Theatre of the London Fairs in the Eighteenth Century* (Cambridge, 1960).

Conclusion

'A playhouse,' said Thomas Earl, 'is the Epitome of the World.'[1] If we add the patent houses to the Opera House, we can certainly make something that is an epitome of the artistic life of London in the mid-eighteenth century. They were centres for the study of the art of elocution, scene-design, acting, ballet, and singing in opera and oratorio. Topical verse was recited from the boards in prologues and epilogues. Copies of plays and word-books were for sale at performances.

The patent theatres were meeting places for all classes from the King down to the criminal, and the nobleman to the footman. Audiences had a high sense of their collective dignity, but were good-tempered unless aroused by some apparent arrogance on the part of managers or players. Then they acted swiftly, smashed benches and chandeliers, and enforced their will. They also liked exercising their privilege of welcoming or damning a new play, and in their decision gave us the clearest indication of general taste that we can find.

It was very conservative. Almost a third of all the plays given at Drury Lane in the whole of one season were by Shakespeare. Other favourites were by Addison, Steele, Cibber, Vanbrugh, Mrs. Centlivre, Henry Carey, Congreve, Farquhar, Fielding, Gay, Otway and Rowe. The same comedies and tragedies went on appearing year by year. Audiences of the day delighted in

1   *The Country Correspondent* (1739), p. 22.

humour and satire, and were very ready to encourage playwrights who could turn out new sentimental comedies, 'laughing'
comedies, and farces. Those by Murphy, Kelly, Garrick, and
Foote reached a very competent standard, but the best were by
Hoadly, Colman, Goldsmith and Sheridan. In fact these were
the only ones that came to terms with the age and showed it
itself from a particular angle.

'A good Comedy,' wrote Samuel Richardson, 'is a fine
Performance. But how few are there than can be called good?
Even those that are tolerable are so mixed with indecent
Levities and with Double Entendres.' Richardson was speaking
for a thoughtful section of tradespeople that was becoming
very influential. It felt that a dissolute stage represented a
debauched society, and that patrons of the theatres should
make known their detestation of Restoration comedies and
other smutty plays. Consequently, in 1750, 'A Student of
Oxford' was able to report that 'since Mr. Garrick's Management, the Stage is become the School of Manners and
Morality; Ribaldry and Prophaneness are no longer tolerated.
Sense and Nature exert their Influence; *Pantomime* daily de-
clines; Dancers are little encouraged; the *Burletta* performs to
empty Benches, and the *British* can now vie with the *Athenian*
Drama, when in its Severest State of Purity.'[2] The student was
rather optimistic in thinking that pantomime was dying: it grew
more and more spectacular until it was taken over by speaking
pantomime. Dances, too, went on being given. He was correct,
however, in saying that ribaldry and profaneness were excluded
from plays and that a delight in didactic sentiments was general.
In the sixties and seventies, the stage seemed very moral in its
outlook, though the playhouse itself could hardly be said to be
in a state of purity. In fact, much of the opposition to the theatre
was caused by the presence there of whores in the boxes and
galleries. They were so numerous that the parts they frequented
were called 'the fleshmarket'.

Yet many people were very proud of their patent theatres,

2 *A Dissertation on Comedy* (1750), p. 15.

and Goldsmith expressed a common feeling when he declared that their magnificence was 'far superior to any others in Europe where plays only are acted.' He noted the great care London performers took in painting their faces for a part, 'their exactness in all the minutiae of dress, and other little scenical proprieties.'[3] As everyone knew, Drury Lane under David Garrick was very highly disciplined. Covent Garden was not quite so efficient, but in singing and pantomime its standards were unsurpassed.

An affectionate interest in the theatre also led Goldsmith to mention one 'impropriety'; 'As, for instance, spreading a carpet punctually at the beginning of a death scene, in order to prevent our actors from spoiling their cloaths; this immediately apprizes us of the tragedy to follow; for laying the cloth is not a more sure indication of dinner than laying the carpet of bloody work at Drury Lane.'[4]

The practice of putting down the tragedy carpet developed out of the need to protect the costumes when an actor or actress fell in death or mad scenes. Much was made of these occasions. 'Gentleman' Smith's death throes as Richard III were described as 'flounder-like'.[5] Mrs. Bellamy contented herself by saying that when she came to the mad scene in *The Earl of Essex*, she threw herself upon the floor 'as usual.'[6]

Although the actors constantly appealed to 'nature' as their guide, it seems very unlikely that their technique was realistic. Compared with the old formal school that Quin belonged to, the methods used by Garrick and Mrs. Pritchard probably seemed very natural, but there is evidence to suggest that it had an artificiality of its own. Garrick was accused of 'starts, jumps, and distortions.'[7] He made points that were greeted with roars of applause. His 'turns' were famous; 'attitudes' seem to have been frequent.

---

3 *Collected Works* (*ed. cit.*), i. 361.   4 *Ibid.*, i. 362.
5 *Morning Post*, 1 November 1779.
6 *Apology* (2nd ed., 1785) iii, 61.
7 *The Theatrical Examiner* (1757), p. 24.

Yet the impression he made on his audiences was of an immediate but surprising sense of reality. He thought it his first business to study the mind and motives of the character he was playing. The method of revelation followed after.

Garrick's professional interests were really those of several other great artists of his day. The seven volumes of Samuel Richardson's *Clarissa* (1748) examine minutely the heroine's psychological reactions, and the nine volumes of Sterne's *Life and Opinions of Tristram Shandy* (1759–67), reveal the close relationship of emotion and the association of ideas. In 1762, Boswell commenced that exercise in self-scrutiny and self-regard that he called his 'Journal'. Garrick was equally interested in perceiving the way the mind worked, but had to demonstrate its processes in action.

It is hardly surprising that he found in Shakespeare's plays the greatest challenge to his imagination. There, motive was to be revealed in a thousand associated touches or images, and character brought out in a great variety of movements, gestures, and looks. Garrick learned 'the art of magnifying trifles'.

Sometimes the effects he achieved were cheap, and we do not easily forgive him for tampering with Shakespeare's text and adding 'strong' speeches. Yet many of his faults, of tinkering with a text or hesitating over a reform, were caused by his realisation that he had to please the public if his theatre was to survive. It was a hard task-master, sometimes even demanding (as on the occasion of *The Chinese Festival*) unconditional surrender. Yet he was usually sensitive to public taste and quick to satisfy its unspoken demands.

It has even been suggested that the intellectual questioning which marked the Restoration and eighteenth century found expression in the theatre in Garrick's attempts at pictorial realism in staging plays.[8] This point of view can be defended, but it seems to me to imply that he consciously evolved an

8 A. Nicholas Vardac, *Stage to Screen, Theatrical Method from Garrick to Griffith* (Cambridge, Mass., 1949), p. xvii.

aesthetic theory that he applied to his work constantly throughout his career.

Clearly strong visual effect was among his aims. Superb miming was an accomplishment that he shared with his rival manager at Covent Garden, John Rich, and pantomime was described in an excellent eighteenth-century phrase, as 'a sort of eye poetry'. Garrick's movements were also a joy to watch and he probably deserved, as much as the ballet-master, Gallini, a tribute to his gestures as 'gesticulated wit'.

As far as stage sets are concerned, he certainly gave De Loutherbourg freedom to experiment with all kinds of vivid effects at Drury Lane in the seventies. In search of novelty, Garrick also brought in people from the street to act as townspeople at Stratford-upon-Avon, and he showed an audience inside Drury Lane Theatre the remarkable sight of a bonfire in Drury Lane. These were tricks to captivate for the moment but in the later history of the theatre they were to become part of the movement towards naturalism.

It must not be forgotten, however, that he showed little practical interest in pictorial realism in costume. He owned books that would have enabled him to attempt historical exactitude if he had wished to do so, but he made only the faintest moves in that direction and they seem to indicate a mere desire for local colour.

After his initial success on the stage, Garrick proved to be very cautious. He made changes in the theatre's lighting and in his last season, had Drury Lane playhouse altered and improved by Adam, but these ventures were dictated by wholly practical considerations. The evidence that he favoured pictorial realism remains slight, and no safe judgement is possible.

The English theatre in the Age of Garrick was one of great acting and a real interest in music and spectacle. It produced no remarkable tragedy, and few splendid comedies; yet, in spite of this, the London theatres were for many years the envy of the world.

Reading List

The most comprehensive accounts of theatrical life in London in this period are unquestionably the relevant volumes of *The London Stage* (Carbondale, Ill.): Part 3: *1729–47* (ed. A. H. Scouten, 2 vols., 1961) and Part 4: *1747–76* (ed. G. W. Stone, Jr., 3 vols., 1962). They print full calendars of performances with much supplementary detail, and excellent introductory sections.

On Garrick himself, the reader will also need to see *The Letters of David Garrick* (ed. D. M. Little and G. M. Kahrl, 3 vols., Cambridge, Mass., 1963), F. A. Hedgcock, *A Cosmopolitan Actor. David Garrick and his French Friends* (1911), and *Private Correspondence* (ed. J. Boaden, 2 vols., 1831). K. A. Burnim's *David Garrick, Director* (Pittsburgh, 1961) is a thoughtful study of Garrick's productions based on material in his prompt books. *The Jubilee* is printed by Elizabeth P. Stein in *Three Plays by David Garrick* (New York, 1926).

The most thorough coverage of the plays produced in the period is to be found in Allardyce Nicoll's two volumes, *Early Eighteenth Century Drama 1700–1750* (3rd ed., Cambridge, 1952) and *Late Eighteenth Century Drama, 1750–1800* (2nd ed., Cambridge, 1952). They contain useful handlists of all the plays of the century, and give cross-references to the Larpent collection. For greater detail on the latter, see the helpful *Catalogue of the Larpent Plays in the Huntington Library* (comp. Dougald

201

o

MacMillan, San Marino, California, 1939). F. W. Bateson's *English Comic Drama, 1700–1750* (Oxford, 1929) is an acute critical study of the drama before and at the beginning of our period. Other information may be extracted from the *Bibliography of English Printed Tragedy, 1565–1900* (comp. C. V. Stratman, C.S.V., Carbondale and London, 1966), and from J. F. Arnott and J. W. Robinson, *English Theatrical Literature, 1559–1900. A Bibliography incorporating Robert W. Lowe's A Bibliographical Account of English Theatrical Literature published in 1888* (1970). G. C. D. Odell's *Shakespeare from Betterton to Irving* (New York, 2 vols., 1920) is still very valuable.

Other illuminating monographs on aspects of the subject are Watson Nicholson's *The Struggle for a Free Stage in London* (1906), C. H. Gray's, *Theatrical Criticism in London to 1796* (New York, 1931, repr. 1964), E. W. White's *The Rise of English Opera* (1951), J. J. Lynch's, *Box, Pit and Gallery: Stage and Society in Johnson's London* (Berkeley and Los Angeles, 1953), D. F. Smith's *The Critics in the Audience of the London Theatres from Buckingham to Sheridan* (Albuquerque, 1953), and W. M. Merchant's *Shakespeare and the Artist* (Oxford, 1959).

For the theatre outside London, the reader is referred to the footnotes in the chapter on the subject and, for comparative purposes, to the following: A. Hare, *The Georgian Theatre in Wessex* (1957), C. Price, *The English Theatre in Wales* (Cardiff 1948), W. S. Clark, *The Irish Stage in the County Towns* (Oxford, 1965), and Esther Sheldon, *Thomas Sheridan of Smock Alley* (Princeton, 1967).

Index